Clues from the Past

Robin Place

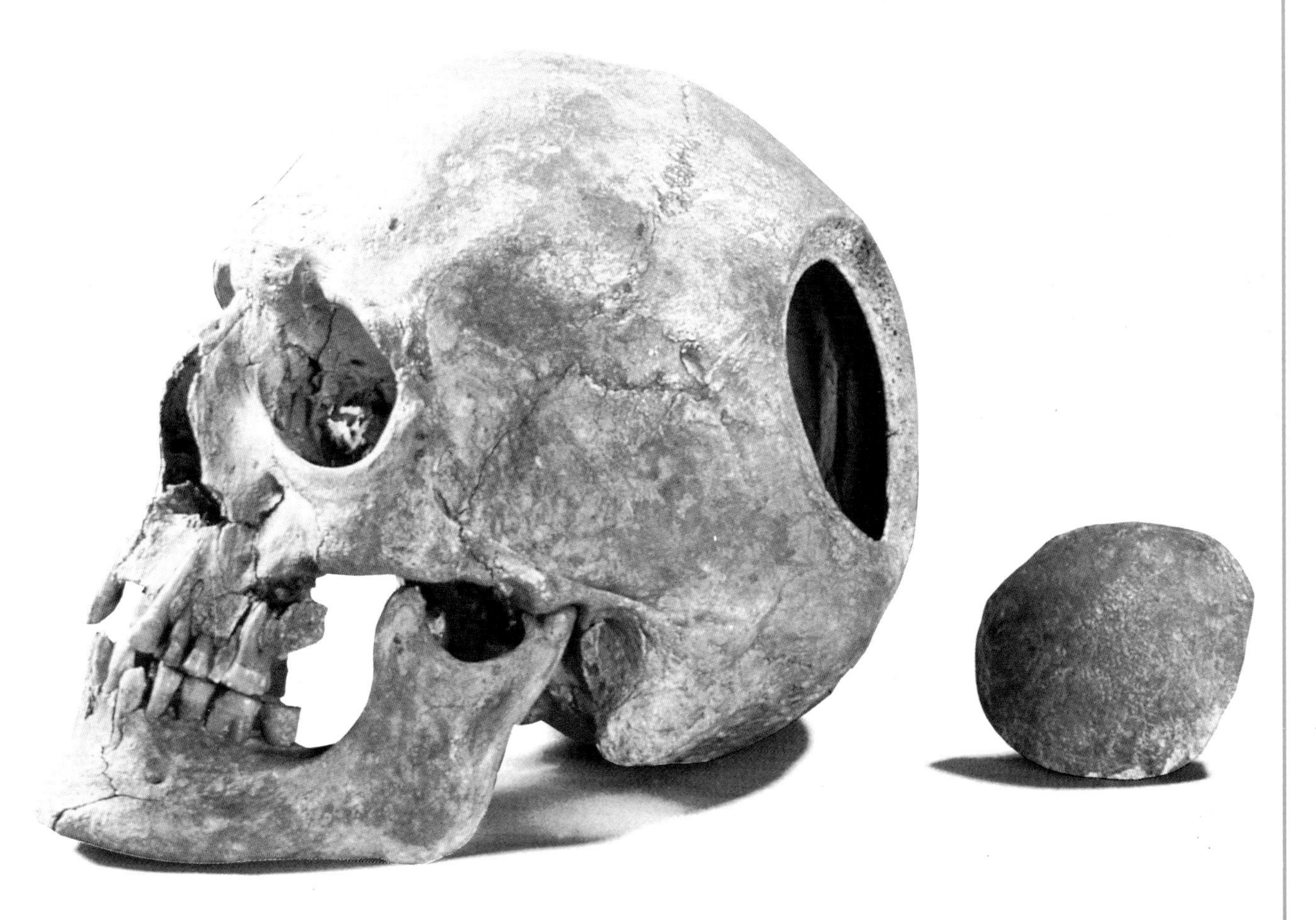

Wayland

Clues from the Past

Editors: Judy Martin/William Wharfe
Designer: Robert Wheeler

Front cover: (clockwise from top right) neolithic flint arrowhead set in wooden shaft, found in Aberdeen; a Roman cavalryman's bronze and iron helmet (first century AD) found at Witcham, near Ely, Cambridgeshire; medieval poulaine, found in London; late neolithic pottery fragment with marks known as the 'Peterborough' style (common in pottery from southern Britain dating from 2800 to 2200 BC).
Back cover: studying a bedbug on a computer microscope in the Archaeological Resource Centre at York.
Title page: a Bronze Age skull found at Crichel Down in Dorset. See page 11.

Picture acknowledgements
The publishers gratefully acknowledge the permission of the following to use their photographs as illustrations in this book:
Roy and Lesley Adkins 36 (bottom); Ashmolean Museum, Oxford 37; British Museum *cover* (centre), 26 (right), 27, 29, reproduced by courtesy of the Trustees of the British Museum; J. M. Coles 30; Devizes Museum 35 (right); Eye Ubiquitous (Geoff Redmayne) 41; Fishbourne Roman Palace 36 (top); Dr L. Hurcomber/Dept. of Prehistory and Archaeology, University of Sheffield 22; Michael Holford *cover* (top left) (Museum of Archaeology and Anthropology), 11 (right), 45; Ironbridge Gorge Museum 44; Alexander Keiller Museum, Avebury 14 (bottom), 15; Robin Place 9, 10, 13 (bottom); Museum of London *cover* (bottom), 17 (left), 19, 21, 31, 32, 33, 42, 43 (left); Nigel Macbeth/Sutton Hoo Research Trust 5; W. Oliver 23 (bottom); Southampton City Civic Centre 35 (left); Sussex Archaeological Society 38; Winchester Excavations Committee 7 (top and bottom); York Archaeological Trust *back cover*, 4, 12, 13 (top left), 14 (top), 16, 17 (top), 18 (right), 20, 23 (top), 26 (left), 34, 43 (right).
Photographs on pages 13 and 24-25 were taken by Zul Mukhida from finds loaned by Pat Stevens and Robin Place. Artwork was supplied by Stephen Wheele Design Associates. The map on page 3 was drawn by Peter Bull. Symbols at the top left and right corners of each text page were drawn by John Yates.
Artwork on page 40 was adapted from the original by G. K. Beulah. Artwork on page 41 is from information supplied by the Gladstone Pottery Museum. The drawing on page 43 (left) is reproduced by permission of Brian Hobley.
The author and publishers would like specially to acknowledge the valuable assistance of York Archaeological Trust in the preparation of this book.

This edition published in 1995 by Wayland (Publishers) Ltd

First published in 1993 by Wayland (Publishers) Ltd
61 Western Road, Hove, East Sussex BN3 1JD, England

British Library Cataloguing in Publication Data
Place, Robin
Clues from the Past
I. Title II. Wheele, Stephen 936.1

HARDBACK ISBN 0 7502 0677 2
PAPERBACK ISBN 0 7502 1723 5

Typeset in the UK by Dorchester Typesetting Group Ltd
Printed and bound in Italy by G. Canale & C.S.p.A., Turin

Contents

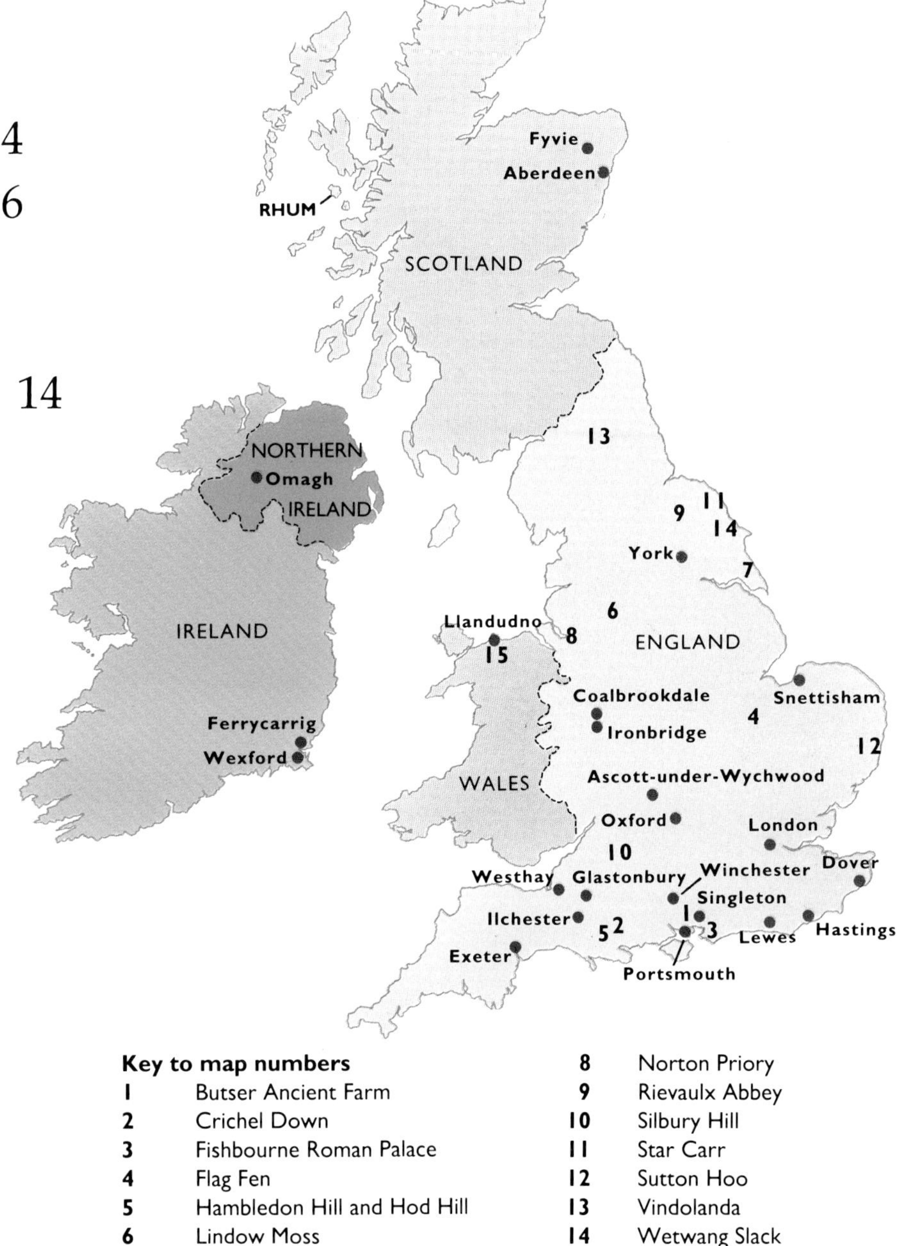

This map shows the place names and archaeological sites described in the text and in the list of Places to Visit on page 47.

Digging for clues

Archaeology is exciting! When a dig begins, archaeologists never know what they might discover. But they are not looking for treasure of gold or silver.

An archaeological find is exciting not because it is valuable, but perhaps because nothing like it has been found before; because of the way it was made; or because it was traded from a distant land to the place where it later became buried. Other finds are exciting because they are made of wood, cloth or leather, which are hardly ever found. These materials decay without trace in dry ground, and are only preserved if they have been kept wet.

Archaeologists' finds are like detectives' clues – clues connected not with a crime, but with how people lived long ago. There are many different kinds of clues.

Looking for evidence

Traces of houses made of wood or stone are important evidence of the kinds of homes people built. If a house was built of wood, the only clues to its construction may be dark marks in the soil. Careful excavation will find the round, dark 'post-holes' that show where the main uprights were sunk into the ground. Archaeologists can discover whether the house was round or square, and how large it was.

They look, too, for tools that people made from flint or rock, or from metals like bronze and iron. Sometimes they can work out what tools people used by looking at the marks left on wood and stone. Some tools we use today are hardly different from those of 2,000 years ago.

Archaeologists also try to find evidence of crafts, like pottery-making. Finds of leather give clues to the history of shoe-making. Pieces of woollen cloth give clues to weaving methods, and the dyes used for colouring yarn and cloth.

By examining human bones, archaeologists find clues to how long people lived, and to some of their diseases. In acid, sandy soil bones do not last long, but at the Saxon burial ground in Sutton Hoo, diggers were trained to

Archaeologists excavating Viking houses in York. White markers show where wooden posts have been found.

A 'sandman' at Sutton Hoo. The dark stain was sprayed with a chemical as it appeared, to make it hard.

follow dark lines in the sand. Careful tracing of the lines brought to light the shapes of bodies – the 'sandmen'.

Animal bones show what animals people kept, and which of them provided meat. Remains of plants and insects found in the soil give clues to the environment long ago.

What is archaeology?

To find the evidence of people's lives long ago, it is often necessary to dig down into the ground. But a dig, or excavation, on site is only a small part of archaeological work. Most of the work takes place afterwards, when the finds are examined by experts.

Geologists identify rocks made into tools; botanists identify plant remains; entomologists study bits of insects. Palaeontologists identify animal bones and anthropologists human bones. Other specialists study cloth, wood and leather finds.

At last, the director of the excavation uses the work of all these specialists to write the excavation report – an account of what has been discovered about the people who lived on the site long ago. The report can be used by other archaeologists to compare that site with their own excavations.

So when archaeologists go home after a dig, it may look as if their work is done. But in fact, it is only just beginning!

Using computers

Computers don't do anything that archaeologists can't do themselves, but they can sort through a lot of information and produce answers to questions very much faster than a person can.

During an excavation, archaeologists are careful to make a plan of the site at every level as they dig down and down. On each plan they mark the exact position of every wall, rubbish pit, well and other main features. They also measure pieces of pottery, coins and other objects in the exact places where they are found. After the dig, the site will disappear, often replaced by a large modern building, so archaeologists can't go back to check up on something they forgot to put on the plan.

A complete record

As the plans are made, the information is fed into a computer. This means that archaeologists do not have to get out lots of paper plans if they want to compare what was found at one level with what was found at another, or see how walls marked on one plan may join up with walls found in another part of the site, perhaps forming one large building. They can call up the different plans quickly on the computer screen, and may find that it is important to start digging in another part of the site to follow up a clue given by the different plans. So using a computer like this helps archaeologists while a dig is going on.

Analysing the data

The excavation report written after the dig is not just a list of everything that was found. The finds are studied to see what they show about the everyday life of the people who made and used them; how well things were made by craft workers; and from how far away goods were brought back through trade with other places.

Using a computer helps in this study. Once the various experts have cleaned and identified all the finds, they record the details of each object in a computer. When the director comes to study the pottery, for example, he or she can call up different analysis programmes, which display on screen, or print out, all the pots made in a certain place or at a certain time, all those that have a particular shape or are decorated with particular patterns. This saves hunting through lots of notebooks or going through a card index many times. The computer does the sorting almost instantly.

Computer reconstruction

Using information from a dig in Winchester, a computer was able to recreate the past. Archaeologists excavating under the cathedral green found the remains of a Saxon monastery church that had been rebuilt several times on the same site. Only the lowest parts of the walls were found.

Archaeologists found the measurements of all the different churches and worked out what each church might have looked like when it was complete, by referring to drawings in Saxon manuscripts.

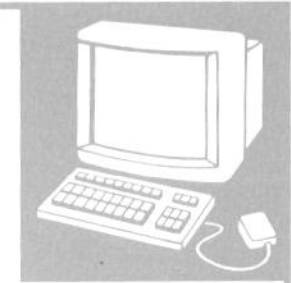

Then a computer was given the data describing all the important points on each different church. The computer joined up the points and presented on screen three-dimensional views of the churches.

The development of the Old Minster, Winchester: computer graphics (below) were constructed from evidence found in excavations. One dig found the chalk foundations (right) of a part of the Minster with curved walls (seen in the third computer reconstruction). The foundations were strengthened with timber beams, the brown lines.

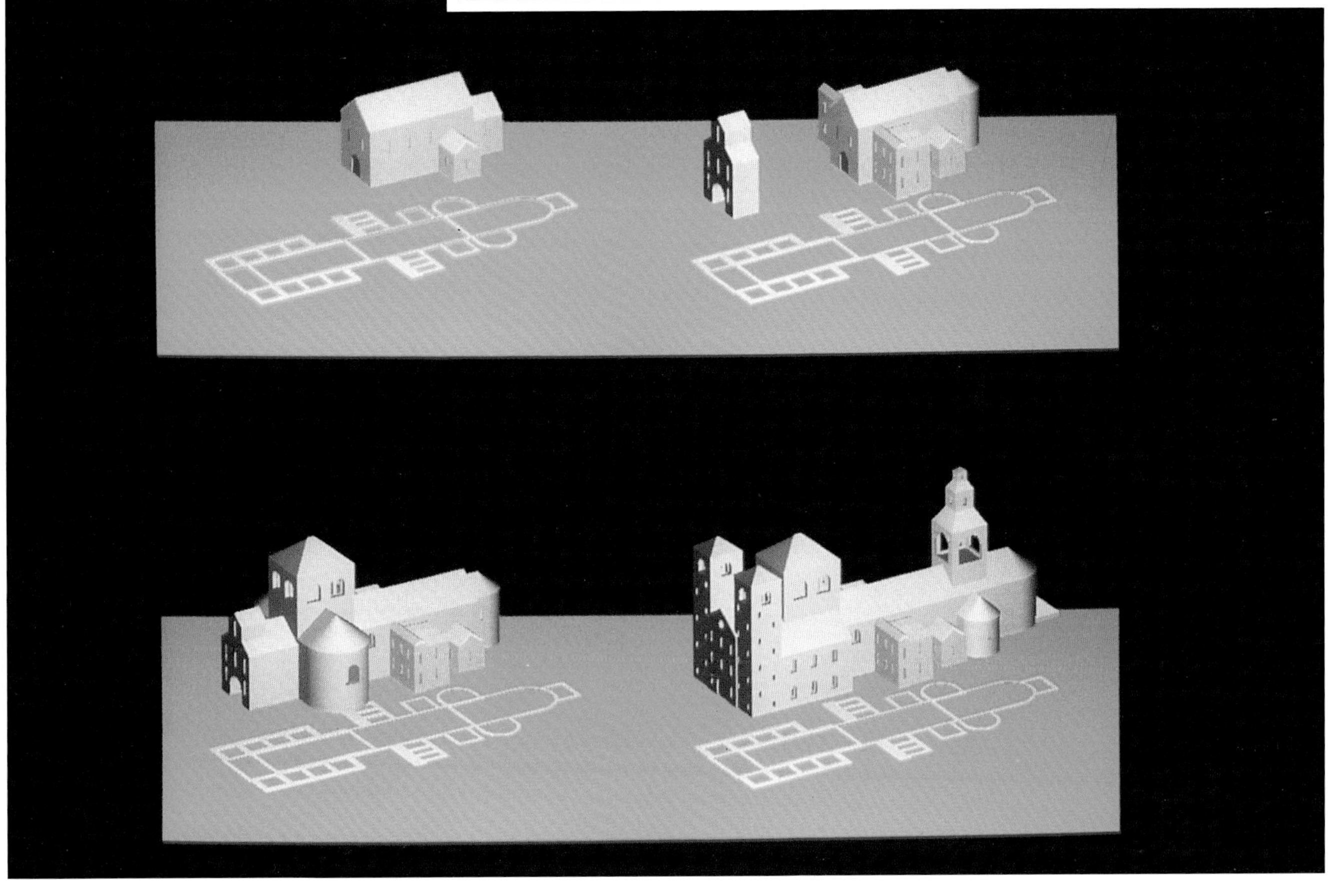

Human bones

Many human bones have been found on excavation sites, sometimes even whole skeletons. They provide a lot of clues about the people of earlier times – what they looked like, how long they lived and how healthy they were.

Archaeologists study human bones for two reasons. They look for traces of disease, because this helps doctors who are studying the history of diseases and trying to cure them. Also, they want to find out all they can, from bones alone, about the appearance and health of the different populations of Britain: Stone Age hunters, neolithic, Bronze Age and Iron Age farmers, Romano-Britons, Saxons, Vikings and medieval people, up to Victorian times.

Finding out about people

If you look at people around you, you will see how different their heads are. Seen from above, the head may be longer from front to back than from side to side, or it may be nearly round. Some people have a long, thin face, others have a broad face. Archaeologists take many measurements on ancient skulls to find the typical shape for each of the ancient populations of Britain.

They also measure the long bones of arms and legs, because from these a person's height can be worked out. Average height in Britain has increased in the twentieth century, due to better health, but before then there was little difference between peoples. Neolithic farmers averaged 1.68m tall; Romano-Britons were 1.70 m. The people who brought bronze-working to Britain 4,500 years ago were a little taller, as were the Saxons.

Male or female?

We can't always be sure whether an adult skeleton is male or female. Usually, men are taller, and have larger bones, with marks left on them by more powerful muscles. But some men are short and lightly built, while some women are tall and muscular. The skull and pelvis show the difference best, but the spongy bone of the pelvis is often too broken to be useful.

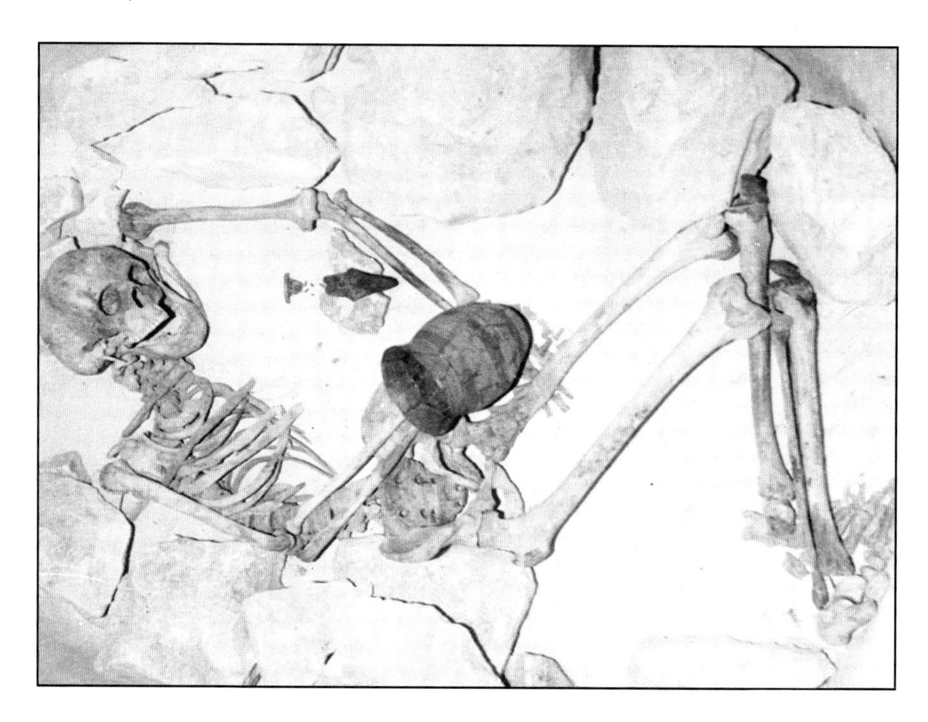

A man buried 4,500 years ago. We only know how people died if disease or a weapon left marks on the bones.

Child skeletons are difficult to sex because the bones of young boys and girls are similar.

How old?
Archaeologists work out how old a person was at death from the state of the bones (old people's bones become light and brittle) and the amount of wear on the molar teeth. Some teeth are so worn-down that only the roots are left in the jaw. For the 6,000 years up to the end of the Middle Ages, they estimate that the average lifespan was 34 years for men, less for women.

If jaws and teeth are found, it is easy to tell the age of a child, by seeing which of the milk teeth have been replaced by permanent teeth. (We assume that children long ago developed their permanent teeth at the same ages that children do today.)

The bones of a young person's skeleton give clues to age. To allow for growing up, the shafts of a child's long bones, and parts of other bones too, are joined to the hard ends by gristle, or cartilage. As the child grows taller, the cartilage is gradually replaced by bone. Using a chart showing this, we can work out how old the person was, up to about 25 years old.

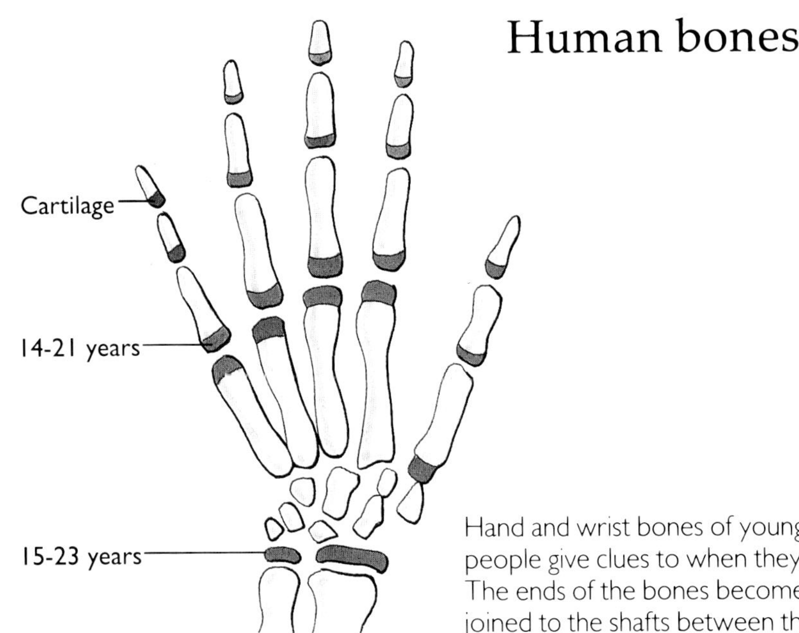

Hand and wrist bones of young people give clues to when they died. The ends of the bones become joined to the shafts between the ages of 14 and 23 years.

Toothache
Archaeologists record tooth decay and gum disease in skulls of different periods. Prehistoric people had a certain amount, but many Romano-Britons had very bad teeth. Saxon teeth were better, but in the Middle Ages sugar was imported to sweeten food, and tooth decay became much worse. Some people lost all their teeth before they died.

Jaw-bone of a neolithic farmer. He must have had bad toothache from the big hole in his back molar tooth.

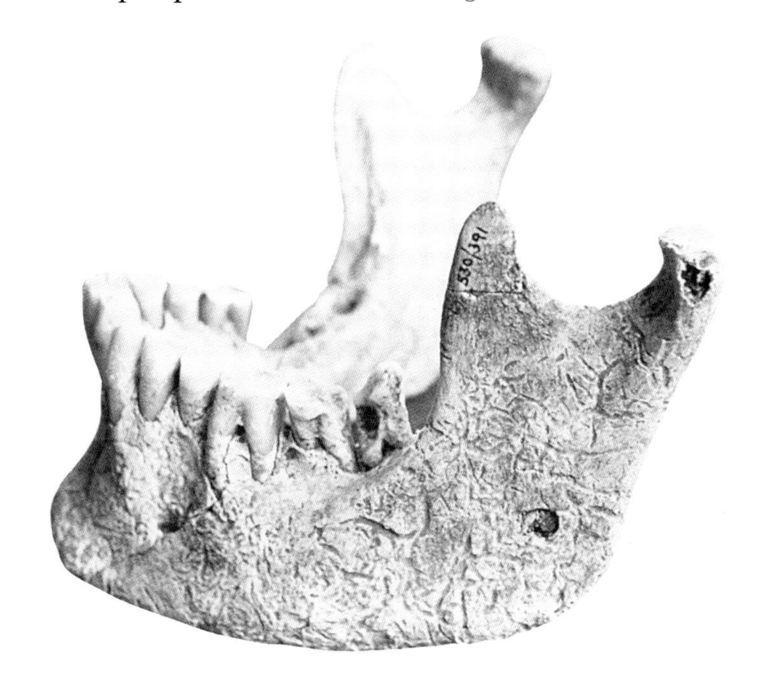

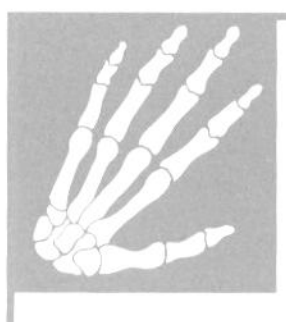

Clues from the Past

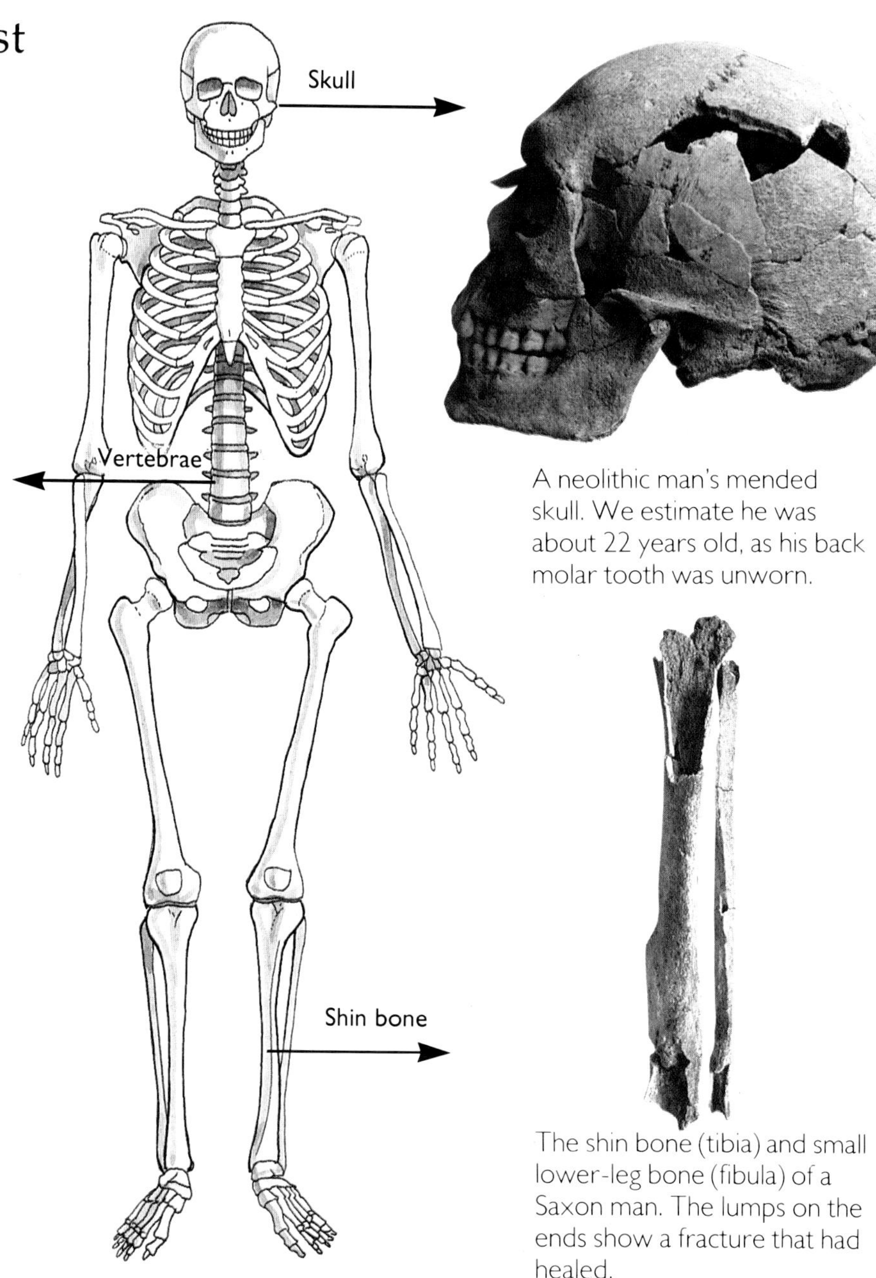

A neolithic man's mended skull. We estimate he was about 22 years old, as his back molar tooth was unworn.

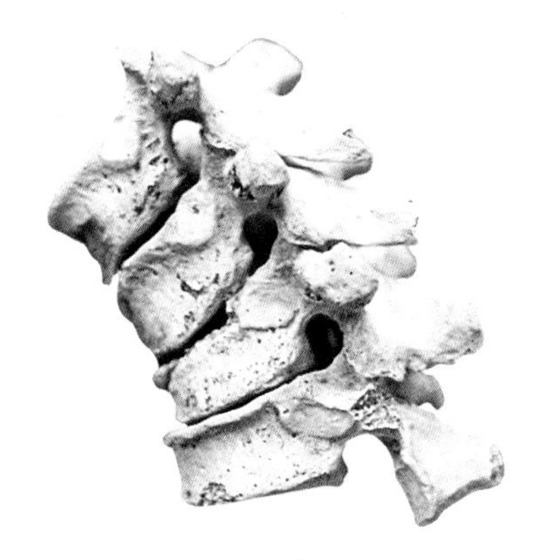

Vertebrae of a neolithic flint miner. The second bone up is narrower than the rest, crushed when the man fell down a shaft. He recovered from the fall.

The shin bone (tibia) and small lower-leg bone (fibula) of a Saxon man. The lumps on the ends show a fracture that had healed.

Accidents and diseases

Accidents are shown by broken bones that healed with a lump of new bone over the break. Skeletons of all periods show fractures in the forearm, when people flung up an arm to ward off a blow. There are many male skeletons with broken shin bones, caused by catching a foot in a plough or stirrup.

Many bones show damage caused by infection after injuries, resulting in diseases. Many people suffered from osteoarthritis, a painful disease particularly affecting the hips, knees and spine. When people lived crowded together in dirty medieval towns, diseases like tuberculosis and leprosy spread. These also caused damage to people's bones.

The thigh bones of a medieval child were excavated in York. Thigh bones should be straight, but this child did not get enough vitamin D from food or sunlight. This weakened the bones and they bent under the body's weight, a condition called rickets.

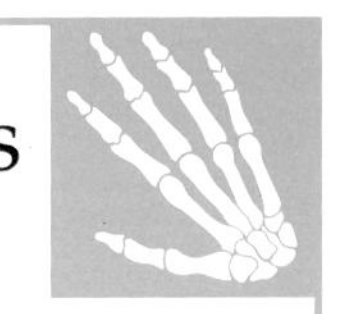

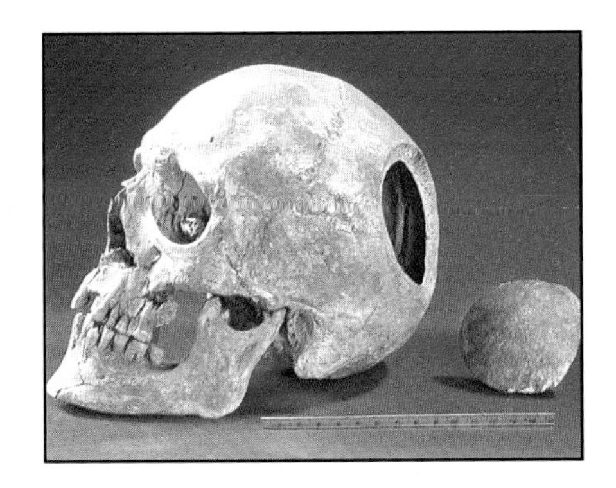

The Crichel Down skull. A sharp flint blade was used to cut out a piece of bone 74 × 66 mm.

A Bronze Age operation

A skull with a large hole cut in it was found at Crichel Down in Dorset. It came from a man who had a twisted spine and must have suffered terrible pain. Perhaps it was believed that the hole would let out the pain. Its sharp edges show that the man died from the operation. In many such skulls, new bone has grown around the hole, showing that the person survived!

Lindow Man

The most exciting human remains are bodies preserved in ice or in peat bogs. In Austria, in 1992, a neolithic 'Iceman' was discovered, with the grass cape he was wearing and a leather rucksack.

Lindow Man was discovered by men digging peat in Cheshire in 1984. He was a Celt, put to death in the first century AD. Archaeologists had to convince the police that the body was not a recent murder victim!

Surgeons and other specialists studied Lindow Man. He was X-rayed. The last meal in his stomach was unleavened bread baked on a griddle. The cut ends of his hair, moustache and beard showed, under a microscope, that they had been trimmed with shears, not with a razor. Although Roman writers said that the Celts painted themselves blue with woad, there were no traces of dye on Lindow Man's skin. He was twenty-five when he died. He may have been a chief, as his well-kept hands showed he had never done manual work.

The body of Lindow Man after cleaning at the British Museum. It has been preserved by freeze-drying. A fingernail is lying on his chest.

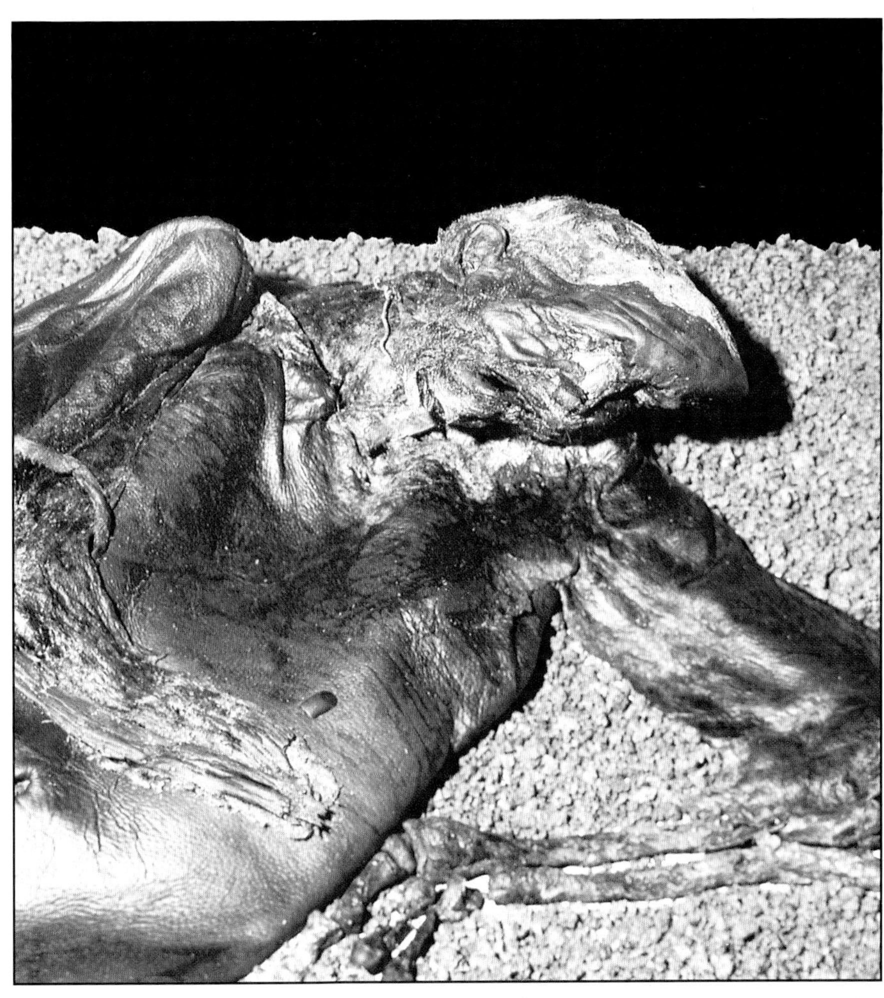

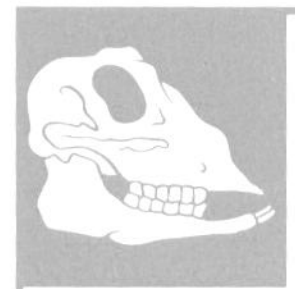

Animal bones

Animals have always played an important part in human life, providing meat, dairy foods, and craft materials like bone and leather, and also helping people with their work.

Animal bones are excavated from sites of all periods. On Stone Age sites, the bones show whether hunters carried a whole animal back to their home after they had killed it, or whether they cut it up and only took home certain joints of meat. Bones are evidence of what people chose to eat, and what animals they kept. In medieval towns, more bones of cattle are found than of other animals, showing that people ate more beef than pork or lamb.

A big problem for archaeologists is that so many animal bones are excavated – 75,000 from five years of digging in Exeter, for example. It takes a long time to identify and list all these fragments from ancient meals, and put the list into a computer.

How old?

How old an animal was when it died is important. Archaeologists want to know whether animals were kept for their milk and wool, and allowed to live to old age; or kept to be eaten, and killed young. Bones from many old cows were found at Hambledon Hill, Dorset. Were neolithic people dairy farmers 5,000 years ago?

Fish dishes?

From the kinds of sea-fish bones found in some sites, we can tell whether people fished from the beach, or caught deep-sea fish in nets cast from boats. Bones of freshwater fish give clues to the state of rivers. Romans who lived in York caught shad, a fish related to the herring, in the river Ouse. But very few shad bones are found in medieval levels – at that time the river was too polluted for them.

Clues to trades

Every piece of bone is washed and examined in case it was used for some purpose – as a tool-handle, for example. Dumps of only one kind of bone give clues to a craft practised nearby. A pile of deer antlers in York marked the workshop of a Viking comb-maker. A pile of long-bones may identify the workshop of a medieval maker of knife-handles. Dumps of horn-cores from cattle show where medieval craftspeople stripped the covering of horn from the core to make spoons, and other household objects.

The brown bone is part of the lower jaw of a shad, found in a rubbish heap in York. The fish had been eaten by someone living in York in Roman times. The white bone is part of a modern shad. Archaeologists keep bones of many animals, birds and fish to help them identify ancient bones.

Animal bones

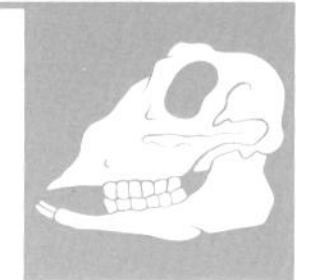

Part of a cow's rib, with a carved design found when the bone was washed. A Viking craftsman used this flat bone as a sketchbook and carved the pattern of an animal with a long, thin body and twisting legs.

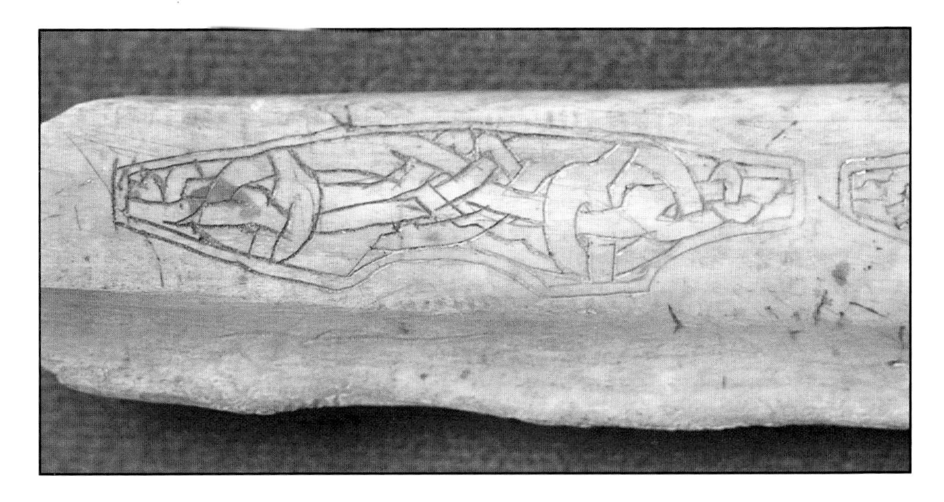

You can learn to identify the teeth of different animals by their size and shape. Each one shown here is a back tooth, a molar.

Horse

Pig

Sheep

Cow

Dog

Our best friends?

The bones of a domestic dog were found at Star Carr, Yorkshire, where hunters camped 9,000 years ago. It is one of the oldest known dogs in the world. The bones show that it was very like a wolf. Skeletons found at neolithic sites 5,000 years old were working dogs that herded cattle. They stood about 52 cm tall at the shoulder and had a broad head with a short muzzle.

In Roman Britain, people kept big hunting dogs and guard dogs – and little lap-dogs too. At Ilchester, Somerset, a grave was found with two skeletons buried side by side – a Romano-British man and his dog.

Many dog skeletons show bones broken by blows and kicks. A medieval dog from York had a broken tail, which had healed with a bony lump growing over the broken bones.

After a dig, bones and teeth have to be identified. This girl is comparing an ancient tooth with the teeth in the skull of a modern horse.

Plants and insects

If we could be carried back in a time machine, would we find the same plants and trees growing in Britain? And would the weather be warmer or colder?

Archaeologists haven't got time machines, but get clues about the environment through history from remains of plants and insects. These also show what kinds of wood people used for fuel and for building houses, what plants they used to make medicines and dyes, and what crops they grew.

Both plants and insects give clues about the climate long ago. In Norman times, a bug that feeds on stinging nettles was common in York. Today, it is common only in southern England. This suggests that in those days Britain was warmer than it is now, because in our own time, the north is generally colder than the south.

Mysterious Silbury Hill

Silbury Hill is the largest man-made mound in Europe. It is 40m high and covers two hectares of ground. Nobody knows why neolithic people piled it up 5,000 years ago. Even the excavations of 1968-70 didn't find the answer.

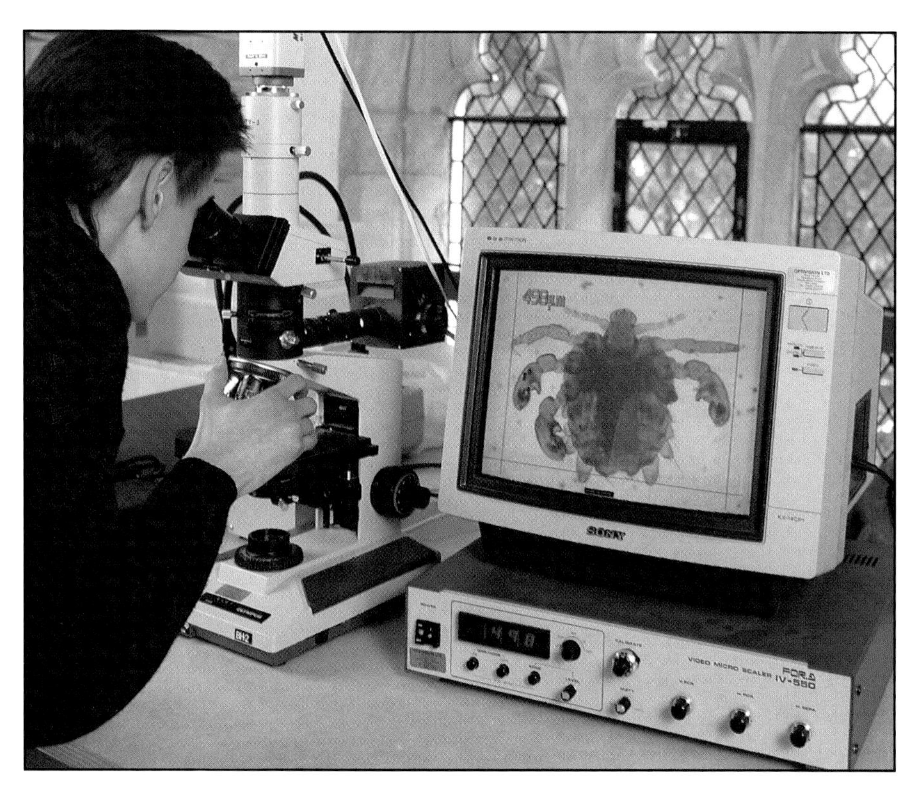

On screen is a modern bedbug, used to identify insect remains. Bugs found in York tell us that Viking houses were not kept very clean.

The kinds of neolithic seeds found under Silbury Hill show that there was grazing land and damp ground nearby, where these plants grew.

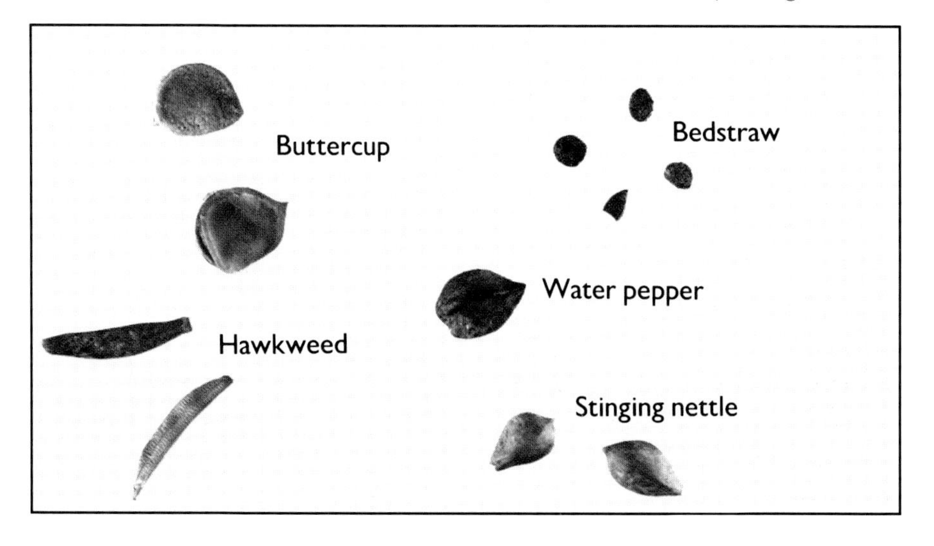

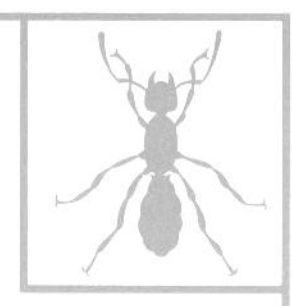

The back (centre) and underside of a neolithic beetle found under Silbury Hill. It is a 'click' beetle, compared here with a modern one (left).

Archaeologists expected to find the grave of a chief at the centre, but nothing like that was there. What they did discover was a mass of turves, 40 m across, heaped over a trampled area in the very centre.

The astonishing thing was that the 5,000-year-old grass was still green, because air had been kept out by the enormous mound of chalk over it. Different kinds of grasses, weeds and insects that once lived in the grass were identified. The excavator said that the ants were so perfect, he half expected them to scuttle away into the nearest crevice.

A Roman storage problem

Beetles have hard armour around the body, and pieces have been preserved and can be identified. Different kinds live in very different places. Dung beetles show places where there was once manure from grazing animals; woodworm beetles show where there were timbers.

In York, a huge number of beetles known to be grain pests were found on the floor of a Roman building constructed in about AD100. There must have been as many as 10 million in the whole building. The beetles showed that the building was a grain store. When grain from that store was moved to Roman forts as army rations, beetles would have gone too, and infected the grain at the forts.

At last the grain store was pulled down and covered with a layer of clay 40 cm thick, burying the beetles. A new grain store was built above the clay. Archaeologists found far fewer beetles in the new building. The storage problem was solved!

Clues to food

Before the invention of flushing lavatories in Victorian times, people used wooden lavatory seats placed over cesspits. In the dark slime of medieval cesspits, archaeologists have found human excrement containing seeds of fruits and bits of leeks, a popular vegetable. Among the fruits that were eaten were bilberries, strawberries, raspberries, blackberries, gooseberries, grapes and figs.

Cloth

At some prehistoric sites in Britain, archaeologists have found traces of fine, thin fabric like linen, made from either flax or nettle stems. But most cloth, in prehistoric and later times, was made of sheep's wool.

The fibres in the yarn give clues to the fleece of the sheep – whether the hair was short or long, and how coarse or fine it was. Long fleeces were used to make the cloth called worsted.

More clues about the fleece come from the study of sheepskins made into parchment for documents in the Middle Ages. The size of the parchment suggests how large the sheep was. Medieval sheep were smaller than present-day breeds. Hairs from fleeces may be found in the surface of the parchment, too. All kinds of wool, from coarse to fine, have been found when these hairs were placed under a microscope.

Coarse and fine cloth that was preserved in wet ground in the Viking town of York.

Cloth manufacture

The yarn used for weaving gives clues to the skill of the people who spun it. Wool fibres from the fleece are pulled out and twisted by the revolving spindle into a single thread, which should be of even thickness. Some cloth made 4,500 years ago was made from very well spun yarn.

By examining cloth, archaeologists can tell whether it was woven on an upright or horizontal loom. In times up to the Middle Ages, women wove at home on upright looms, the warp threads weighted with stone or clay loom-weights. In the Middle Ages, woollen cloth-making became one of England's most important industries. Big horizontal looms, first introduced in the eleventh century, were used in workshops by men.

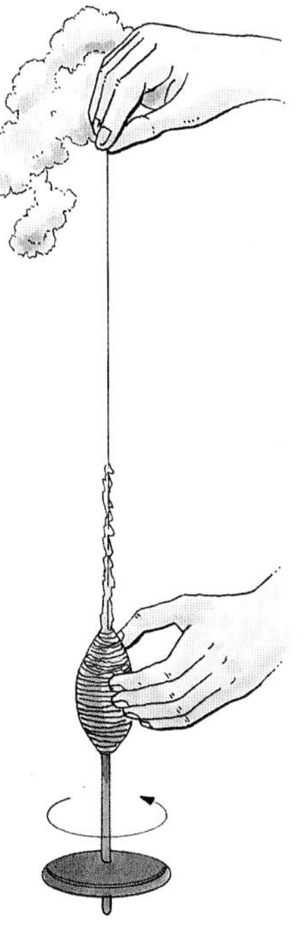

Wool being spun into thread on a spindle, a weighted stick. As the spindle turns, the wool fibres mesh into a continuous thread. Many spindle whorls (weights) have been found on digs.

Colourings and dyes

Some cloth was patterned with natural brown, black and white wools from different sheep, but wool was also dyed. Laboratory analysis of cloth pieces has shown what dyes were used. In prehistoric to Roman times, dyes were made from plants: madder for red and orange: woad for blue; lichens for purple, brown and red dyes; weld for yellow.

In the Middle Ages, dyes were also imported: red kermes, made from crushed insects in Spain; saffron yellow, made from crocuses in India; and purple made from fish in Greece.

Colours change after cloth is buried. Analysis showed that this medieval cloth had been dyed red with madder.

Project

Weaving your own cloth

If you have an opportunity to use a loom, you can weave these patterns, in just the same way as men and women did thousands of years ago.

A model of a Viking upright loom (right). The warp threads are tied to clay loom-weights. Some are looped over a heddle (the centre bar).

Tabby weave
Take the weft (horizontal) thread over and under one warp (vertical) thread at a time. This is the simplest of all weaves, found at all periods back to the early Bronze Age, 4,500 years ago.

Plain twill
Take the weft thread over and under two warp threads at a time. From 4,000 years ago, wooden heddle rods were passed under different threads in each row. Lifting the heddle allowed the weft thread to go under all the right warp threads quickly.

Clues to foreign trade

Coarse cloth made in Iceland was found in the medieval town of King's Lynn, Norfolk, used as wrapping. Silk from China was woven in Istanbul, Turkey, into narrow ribbons, which were bought in Italy by Saxon merchants, and worn by people in London.

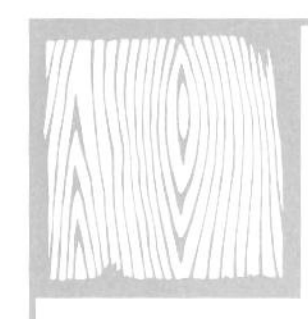

Wood

On many excavations, nothing made of wood is found, because wood rots away in dry ground. But in wet ground, wooden structures and objects survive.

Large wooden structures that have survived include houses, trackways, well-linings and waterfronts. Archaeologists have also found weapons such as bows, arrows and spears, as well as scabbards, tool-handles, household objects such as bowls and cups, pattens (medieval over-shoes worn to keep feet dry on muddy roads), Roman letters written in ink on thin pieces of wood, and even Viking pan-pipes.

Boxwood pan-pipes (above) played by Vikings in York 1,000 years ago. They can still be played – the notes are A to E.

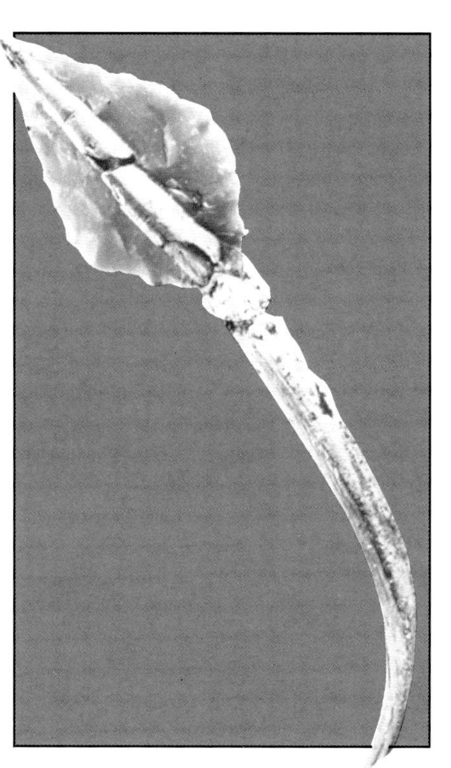

Part of a neolithic arrow found near Aberdeen. It has a wooden shaft and flint head.

How old?

Finds of wood are important for another reason. They can be used to date structures and things found close to them. Wood can be dated by the radiocarbon method, counting radioactive carbon atoms that were absorbed by the living tree, and slowly lost after it was felled.

Another dating method, dendrochronology, involves measuring the yearly growth rings on oak timbers. These vary in width according to the rainfall in each year. Measurements have been collected from oak trees covering hundreds of years up to the present day. Using computers, archaeologists can compare this record with the ring pattern in an ancient block of wood. The best match shows the date when the tree from which the block came was growing.

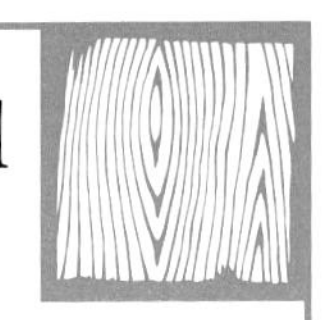

Wooden pattens were overshoes worn in the Middle Ages to keep shoes above the mud in the streets. They were kept on by a leather strap.

In Britain, archaeologists have found trunks of oak trees that grew at different periods of history. The oldest trees were preserved in ancient peat bogs and lake beds. Palaeobotanists (people who study ancient plants) have recorded on computer sequences of tree rings, from modern times back to very ancient times. They have linked trees of different ages by matching groups of very distinctive rings. This diagram shows matched rings (the overlapping sections) at about 1890-1900 and 1870-80.

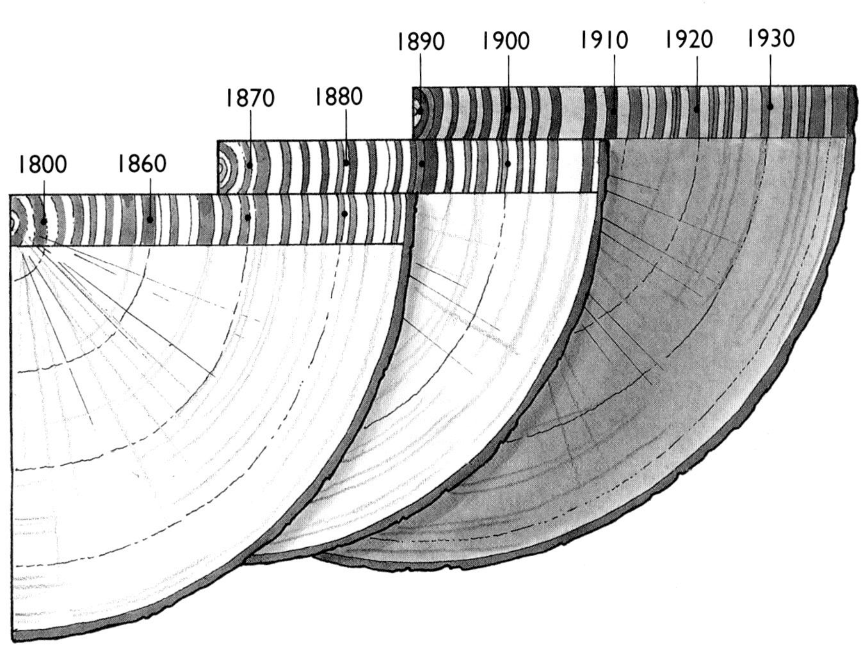

The skill of Roman carpenters

The wooden lining of a Roman well 1.2 m square was excavated in Skeldergate, York. The oak timbers were so well preserved that archaeologists could see exactly how the carpenters had joined the timbers together. All the joints were made by sawing, and an iron nail held each one together. In some joints, small wooden wedges had been hammered in, to give a tight fit.

Dove-tail, half-lap and saddle joints were used for the well timbers. Braces strengthened the corners.

Looking down the Skeldergate well (left). The timbers were built inside a big pit. The space between the timber lining and the pit wall was filled in with soil.

Timbers removed from the well show how the corners were fastened and how braces were jointed in place.

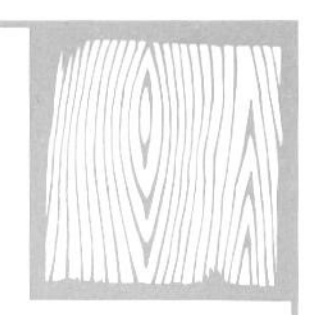

Waterfronts

In Roman, Saxon and medieval times, the people of riverside towns like London and York built massive timber waterfronts, so that ships could tie up at a landing stage instead of having to unload into flat-bottomed barges. Waterfront excavations have provided clues to the size of ancient trees. In London, the Roman waterfront was built of huge oaks 200-300 years old. But so many of these big trees were felled that by the Middle Ages there were none left near London, and medieval waterfronts were built of much smaller trees only 40-80 years old.

Timber must have been in short supply, as old doors and timbers from dismantled ships were built into the waterfronts. The old ships' timbers also give useful clues as to how medieval ships were built. This is important, as very few ships have been excavated.

Building a waterfront in Roman London. Work was done at low tide. The space behind the new timber wall was filled in with rubbish to make solid ground for warehouses. Pottery and coins found in the rubbish tell us the date when this was done.

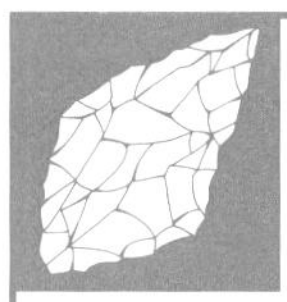

Stones

Some of the earliest hand tools were made of stone and these can often be found without digging. From the shapes of the stones, we know how they were used.

Flint is a stone that can be chipped into sharp tools and weapons. Before people knew how to use metal, they made flint knives for cutting meat, scrapers for cleaning animal skins, saws and sickles, axeheads and arrowheads. Some kinds of rocks were also shaped into axes and hammers by rubbing them smooth on other rocks.

Archaeologists make copies of stone implements, to get clues about how skilful at shaping flint people were long ago.

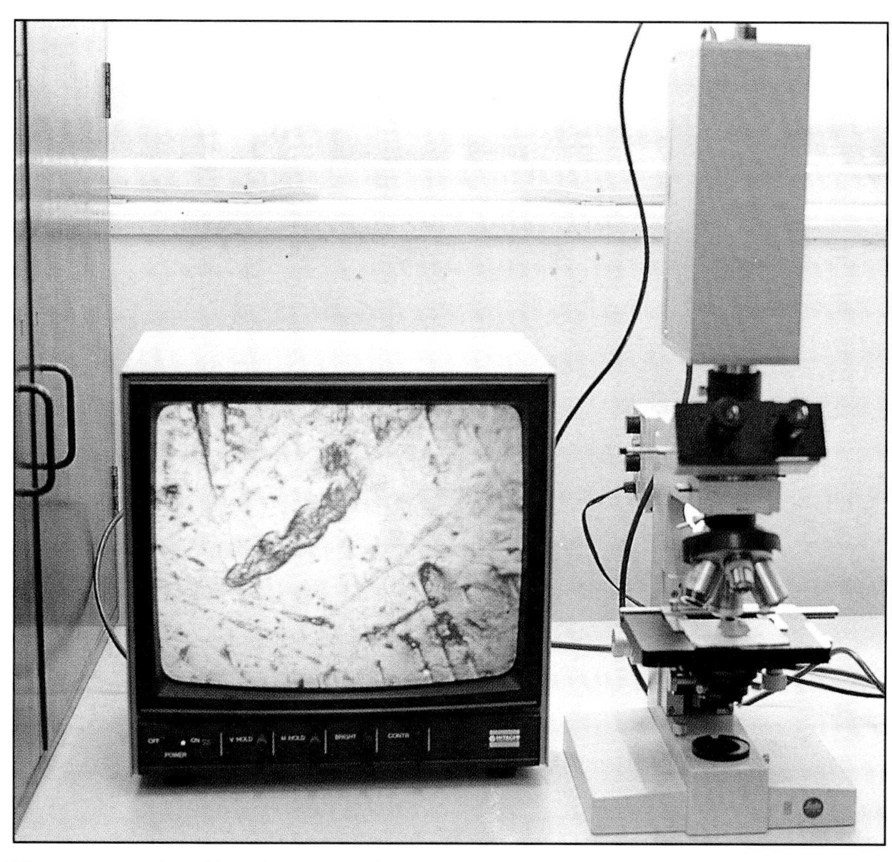

The stone under this microscope is enlarged on the screen to 250 times its real size. Scratches made when the tool was used show up clearly. The tool was found to be polished and shiny, with pieces chipped off at the edges, from being used to cut hard bone.

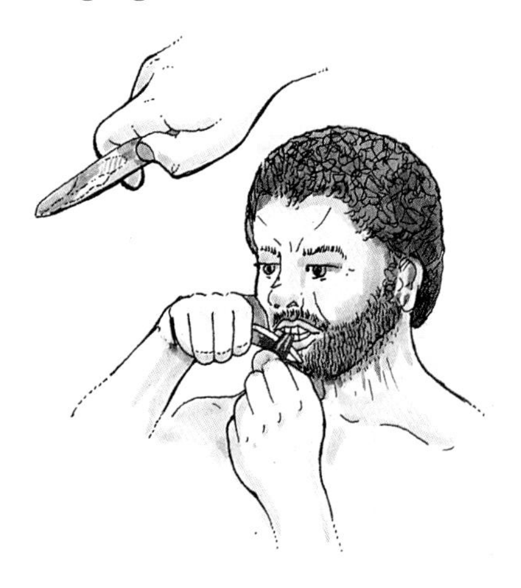

From marks found on flint knives, we know that this is how they were used for eating. People held a strip of meat between their teeth and, with the knife, cut off a bit to chew.

How were tools used?

About 40 years ago the Russian archaeologist S A Semenov started looking at the edges of flint tools under a microscope. He found marks on them left by the ways they were used. He experimented with using pieces of flint to cut wood, bone and meat, and found that each of these things left different marks on the flints. He began to look for similar marks on ancient tools. He found, for example, that a long, thin stone blade was a meat-knife, used to cut off a mouthful of meat.

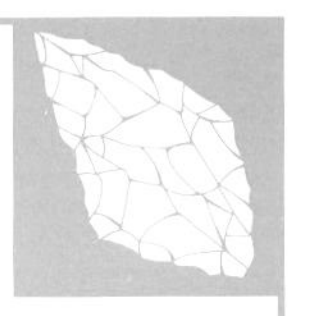

Stone that was traded

Saxon millstones were found near Southwark Bridge in London. This find suggests that there was a watermill nearby. The millstones are made of very hard volcanic lava, a stone that originally came from Germany. Trading of this lava to Britain began 2,600 years ago. It was important to use hard stone for grinding corn so that it did not wear down and cause bits of stone to get mixed with the flour ground from the corn.

Two millstones (left), dating from about AD 1200, found in a cesspit at York. They fell in by accident and no one would get them out. This suggests that a flour mill was sited near a toilet – no wonder there was a lot of disease in those days.

(Below) Using a neolithic grindstone (a quern) to grind corn into flour. The upper stone was pushed to and fro.

Project

Looking for flints
Archaeologists walk over ploughed fields (with the farmer's permission) to look for flint tools and other traces of where people lived in the past. You may be able to join a fieldwalking group organized by your local museum. Here you can see some of the tools to look out for.

In making one flint tool, hundreds of flakes were struck off, so you are more likely to find a waste flake than a tool that the maker took away to use. But waste flakes may show where people made tools. The clues to look for are the flat 'striking platform' and the curved 'bulb of percussion'. Flint does not break flat, like a slate – a blow produces a curved shape. Some flakes were trimmed for cutting or scraping. Look for tiny chippings along the edges of the flake.

Core (below)
People who used flint to make tools shaped a lump so that they could strike off a lot of flakes or sharp blades from it. The lump is called a core. You can see where a blade has been struck off.

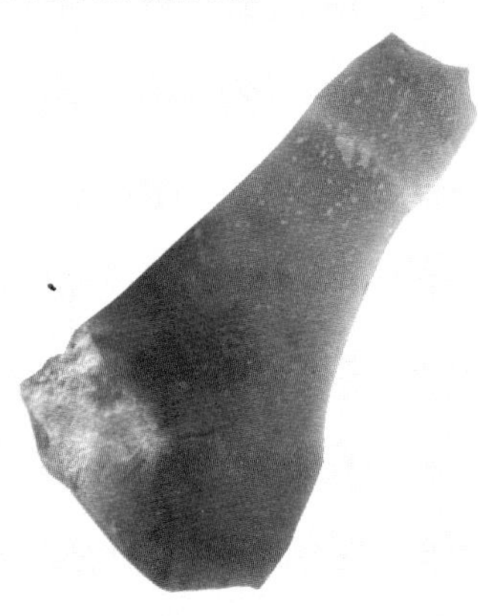

Waste flakes (right)
On both of these flakes you can see the striking platform and the bulb of percussion which spreads out behind it.

Fire-crackled flint (right)
Some prehistoric pottery was not hard enough to stand over a cooking fire. The pot was placed in a hole in the ground and packed round with hay or soil. Pebbles were heated in the fire and put in the pot to cook a stew. Putting a hot pebble into cold water gave the stone a crackled surface.

Scraper (above)
These tools were needed to scrape animal skins being used to make clothing. A flake was struck from a core, and one end or one side was trimmed.

Hand-axe (right)
A very old, all-purpose hand tool from over 250,000 years ago. The pointed end was used to dig up roots. The other end was a hammer for smashing bone to get out the tasty marrow. The sharp sides were used to cut meat.

Polished axe (below)
The first farmers needed axes to clear forest to make fields. These were chipped into shape and rubbed on a rock to smooth them. They have a shiny, polished surface and a straight edge. They were hafted in a wooden handle.

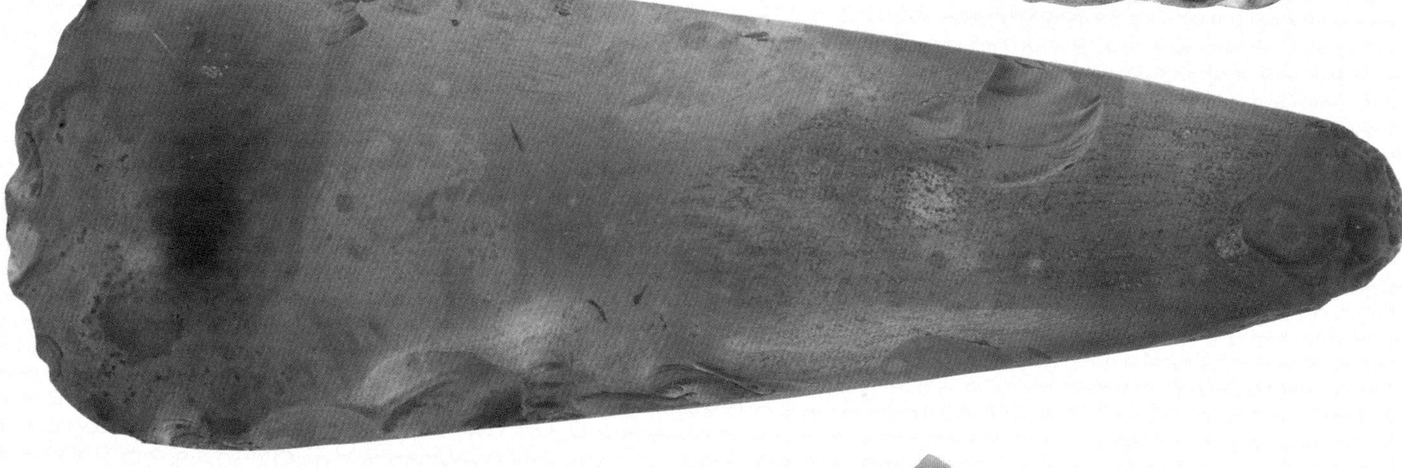

Microliths (above)
Hunters in Britain before farming began used several tiny flakes fitted into a wooden shaft as an arrow or spear. These are microliths, which can be smaller than your fingernails. Some are shaped as crescents or triangles.

Arrowheads (above)
These were shaped by pressing off tiny bits from all over a thin flake of flint, using a tool of wood or deer antler. The neolithic farmers in Britain used leaf-shaped arrowheads (left). In the Bronze Age, barbed arrowheads were made (right).

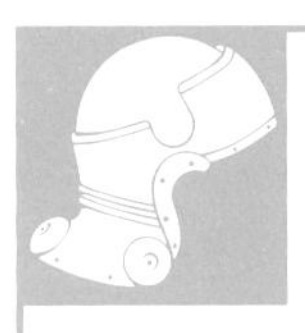

Metals

Metals such as copper, bronze, iron, lead, silver and gold were used by craftspeople long ago. Archaeologists study the tools, weapons and jewellery they made to find out how metalworking has changed between the Bronze Age 4,500 years ago and the present.

The surface of many metal objects is covered with rust and other forms of corrosion after long burial in the ground. To examine a find carefully, it may be necessary to take an X-ray photograph, which can show what lies underneath the damaged surface layer. Inlaid patterns on the Roman dagger sheath shown on the right were revealed only when the sheath was X-rayed.

Conservators work on cleaning and preserving metal in a laboratory. They can clean off corrosion on metal using a Vibratool, a tiny chisel that knocks off small pieces. The X-ray photograph is a useful guide for their work.

A Roman dagger sheath made of bronze inlaid with a pattern in silver. When found, the design was hidden by corrosion, but the design was revealed by X-ray and the corrosion was removed.

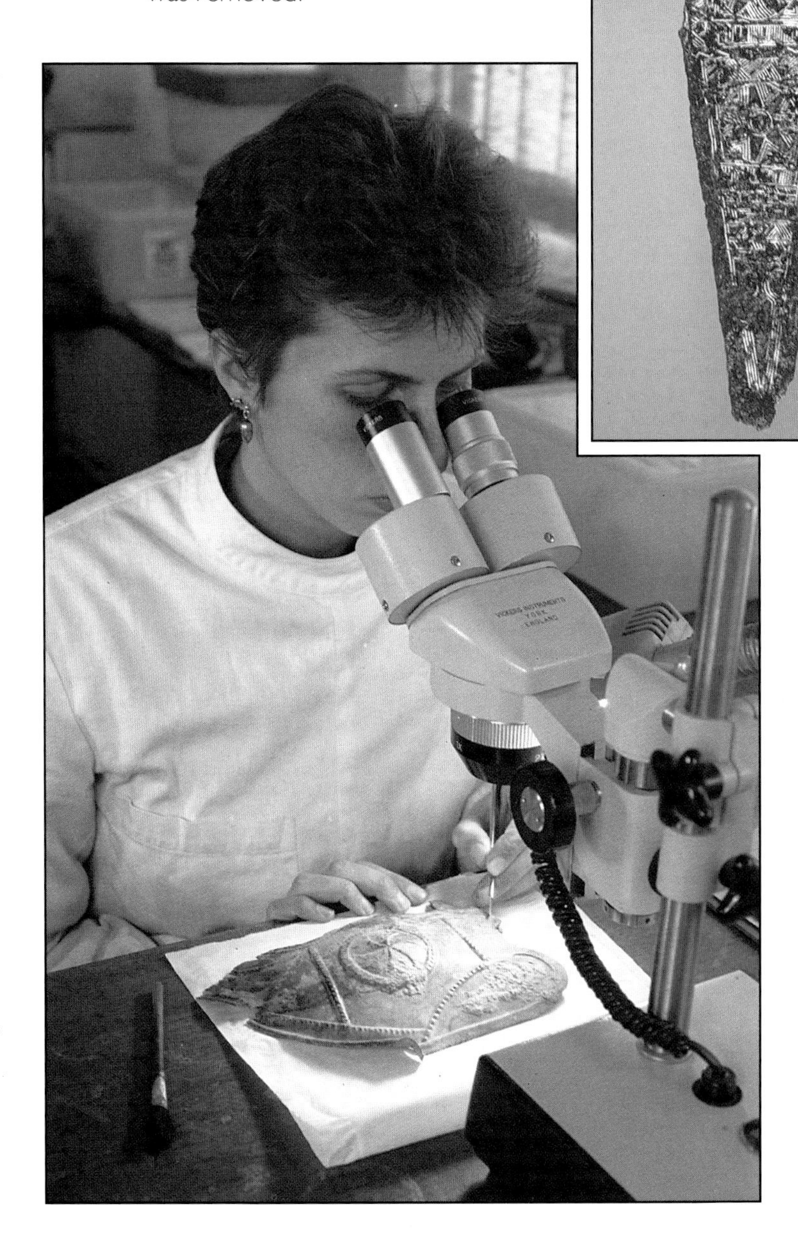

This conservator has nearly finished cleaning part of a Roman helmet. She is using a sharp scalpel and a soft brush to remove the last bits of corrosion, being very careful not to scratch the surface. She is looking into a binocular microscope, which enlarges the area she is working on. After cleaning, the surface of the metal will be treated with chemicals to protect it from further corrosion.

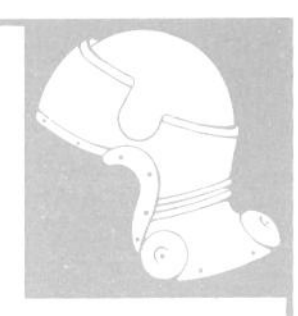

Decorative metalwork

Celtic chiefs, both men and women, wore twisted gold neck rings called torcs. Archaeologists and modern goldsmiths have made copies to find out how torcs were made.

One example was a torc found at Snettisham in Suffolk. The central part was made from eight twisted strands. Each strand was made from eight twisted wires. The ends, worn in front, were modelled in beeswax and fixed to the central part, and patterns were cut into the wax. Then each end was covered in clay to make a mould. The moulds were heated, so the wax melted and ran out. Molten gold was poured into each mould and left to cool and set hard. When the clay moulds were broken open, the golden torc was complete.

A neck ring, or torc, from Snettisham. Many gold and silver torcs were buried there, as a store of metal to be melted down and used again.

Celtic craftspeople drew beautiful patterns on bronze helmets and shields for warriors, and on the backs of bronze mirrors. Archaeologists and modern craftspeople have worked out which tools the ancient metalworkers used from the marks they left on the objects.

Iron Age chariots

Archaeologists have found graves where a man, or a woman, was buried with a chariot. The chariots were mostly made of wood, which has rotted away, but we have some clues from the metal parts which have been preserved in the graves.

The iron tyre, a band around the outside of the wheel, shows the size of the wheel. The nave bands, bronze rings around the central wheel hub, show how big this was. Sometimes the whole chariot was buried in a large grave, with the person lying inside it. The distance between the wheels shows how wide the chariot was.

Other metal objects that have been found give further clues about what the chariot looked like. Rein rings and a pair of bridle bits show that two ponies drew the chariot. The archaeologist Sir Cyril Fox showed that two oddly shaped brooches, which are kept in the British Museum, London, could have been used to fasten a cloth over a pony's back. The Iron Age Celts wove brightly coloured cloth, so the chief in the chariot would have been a fine sight, with the bright cloths over the ponies and the bronze fittings gleaming in the sun.

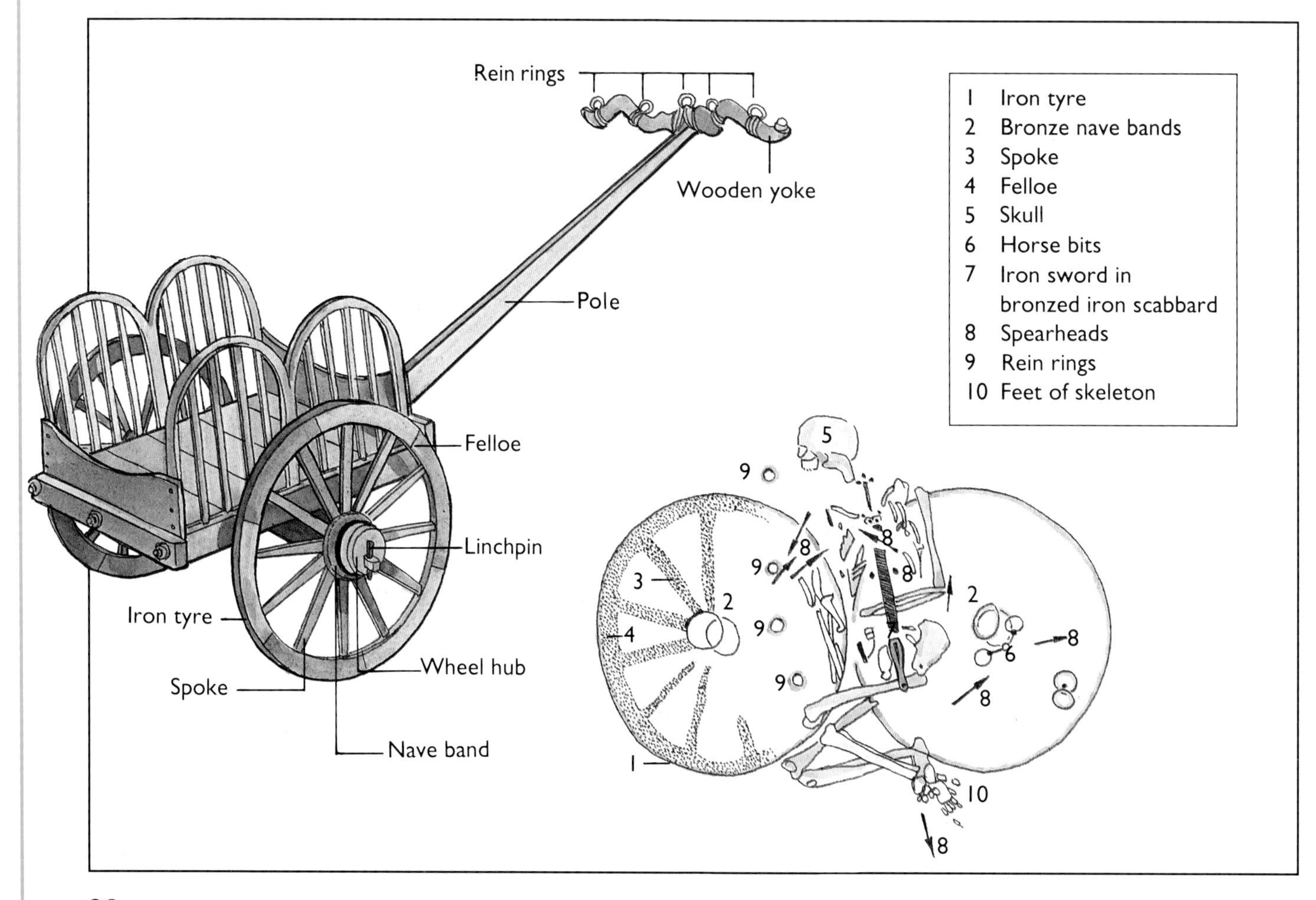

A Celtic chariot, reconstructed from traces found in chariot burials. The diagram identifies the finds in the chariot burial shown opposite.

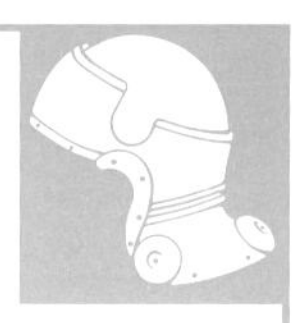

An extra clue

In the grave at Wetwang Slack, Yorkshire (below), the wheels had been taken off the chariot and laid in the bottom of the grave pit. The wheel on the right shows how archaeologists can work out the size of the tyre and the central nave bands, as described above. But as the wood of the wheel on the left decayed, it happened to leave cavities in the ground. The diggers spotted the holes and pumped foamed plastic into them. This revealed the size of the spokes and the felloe, the wooden wheel rim to which the tyre was fixed.

A man buried with parts of a chariot at Wetwang Slack. His body may have been stabbed with spears, so his ghost would not 'walk'.

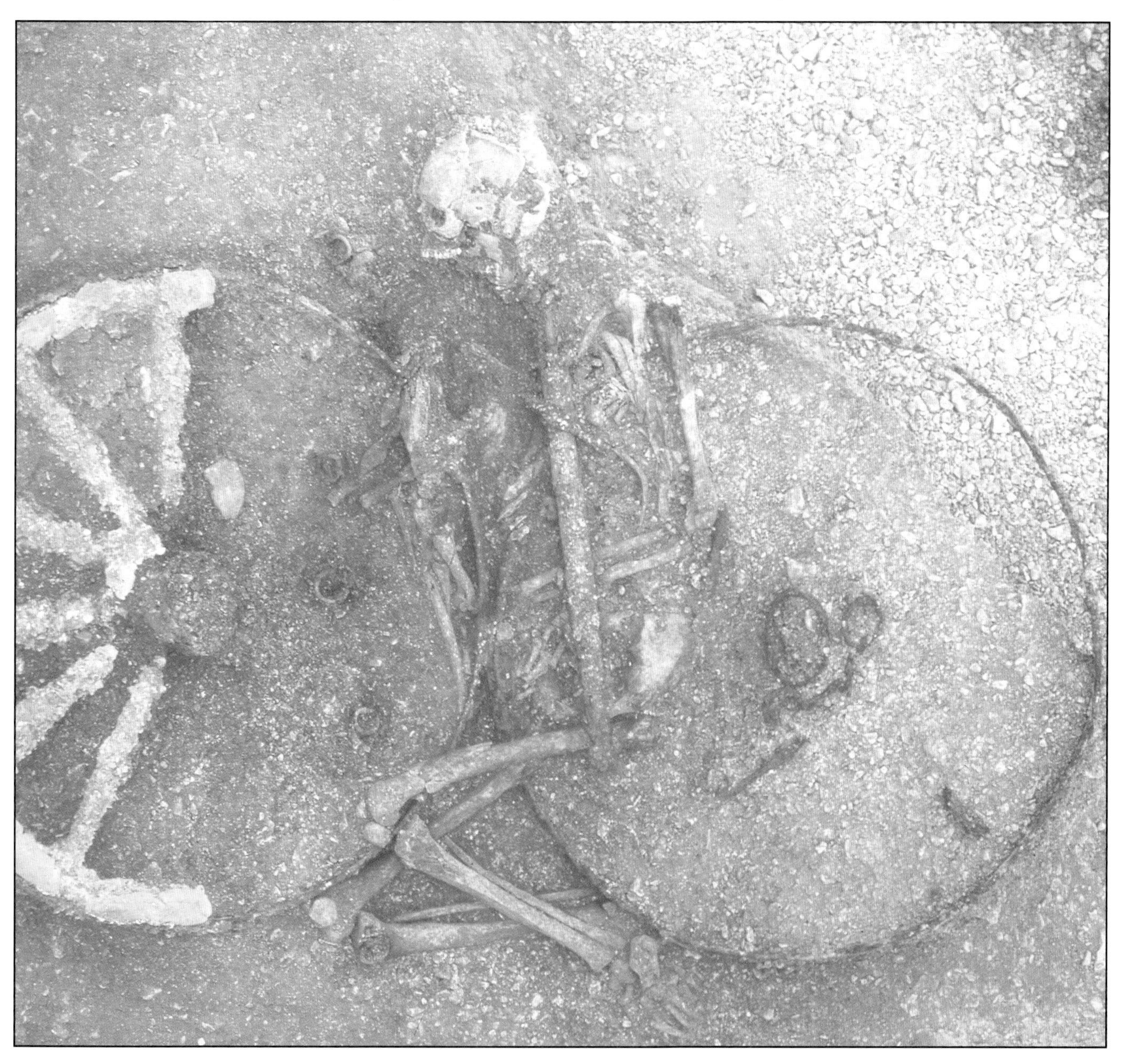

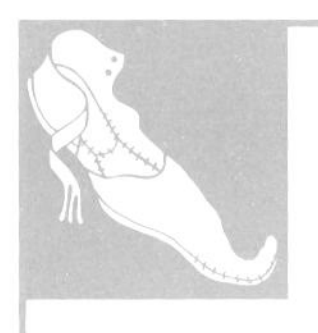

Leather

Animal skins were used to make clothing at least 30,000 years ago. Leather-working tools from prehistoric Britain have been found, although very little leather survives.

Tools made from stone, bone and antlers suggest that prehistoric Britons were able to clean animal skins. Bone needles have been found, probably used for stitching leather. Archaeological finds show that clothing was not the only important use of leather – it was also a good material for certain kinds of weapons.

A neolithic bow

A present-day archer tried out a reconstruction of a yew-wood bow found in Somerset. The original bow was made 4,800 years ago, and is over 1.5 m long. It was strengthened by strips of leather and bindings of thin thread. Using the reconstructed bow, the modern archer hit a target from 60 m.

How strong is leather?

In the late Bronze Age, about 2,800 years ago, round bronze shields were made, but they don't look strong enough to be used in fighting. A leather shield was found in Ireland and archaeologist John Coles thought it was more likely that leather was used to make shields that were taken into battle.

He had part of the Irish shield analysed and found that it was made of cattle skin, tanned with oak bark to stop it going bad. He soaked some cattle-skin until it was soft and hammered it over a wooden mould – one of these was also found in Ireland. To make the shield hard, he dipped it into melted wax – otherwise it would have gone soggy in a shower of rain. Then he demonstrated how a blow from a bronze sword cut right through a bronze shield (he used a copy, not an ancient one), but the sword did not go through his leather shield. The bronze shield may have been made for ceremonies, not for fighting.

John Coles' experiment. His copy of a bronze shield (below) was badly cut by blows from a sword. His copy of a leather shield (right) shows marks made by the sword, but the shield was not cut through.

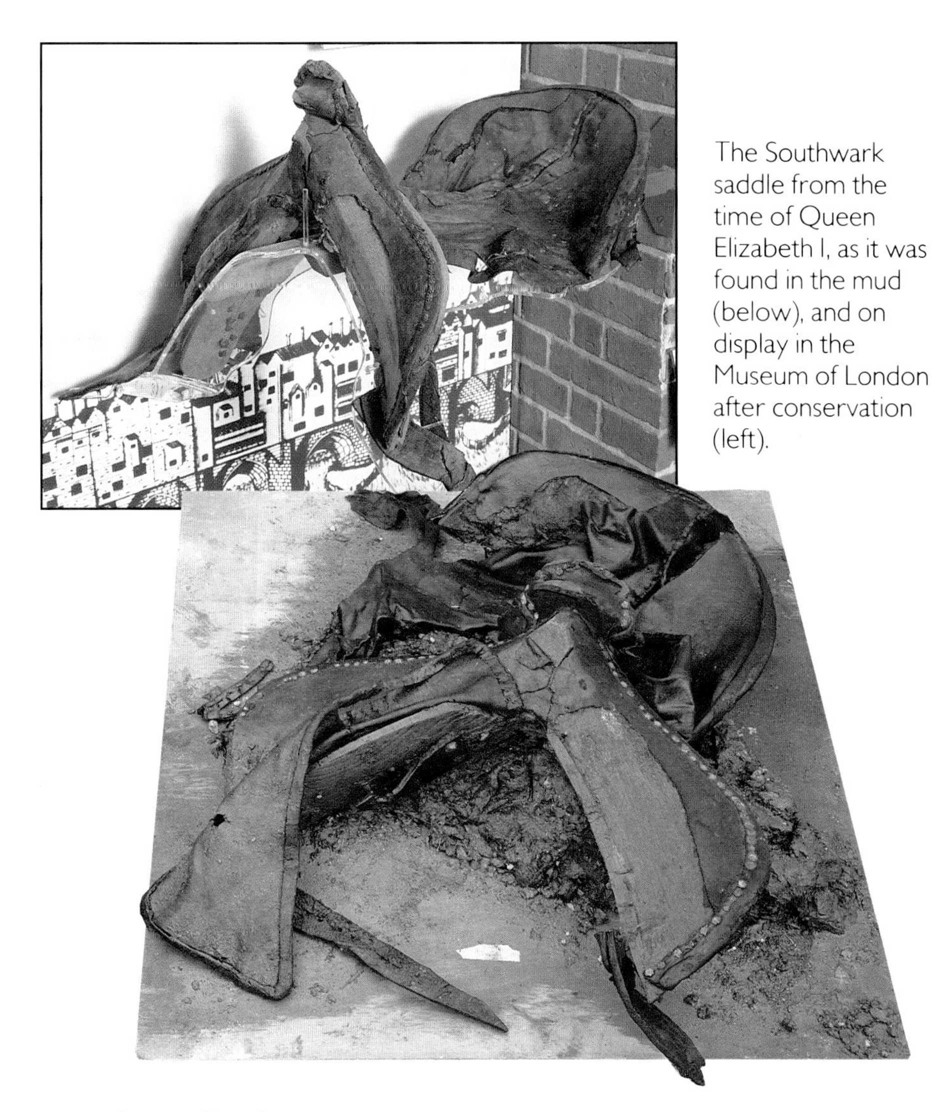

The Southwark saddle from the time of Queen Elizabeth I, as it was found in the mud (below), and on display in the Museum of London after conservation (left).

A unique find

In 1987, archaeologists were excavating in Southwark, on the south bank of the River Thames, opposite the Tower of London. Deep down, they found a big patch of wet ground, the remains of a pond. In the sixteenth and seventeenth centuries, people had thrown rubbish into it. There were many interesting finds that would have rotted in dry ground: wicker baskets, large pieces of cloth, and many shoes. But the most important find was a leather saddle, made about 1600, the only one ever found.

The saddle was not complete. Bits of leather had been cut off, probably to be used for other things. Archaeologists found that the frame was made of beechwood, with a high pommel in front. Over the wood was horsehair padding. The saddle was covered with ox-hide. The edges were bound with strips of leather decorated with metal studs, shaped like flowers.

Shoes

In Roman and medieval Britain, people used leather for making scabbards, purses, harness and many other things, but the only objects that are found in great numbers are old shoes. They were thrown away and have been preserved in wet ground, such as old wells and rubbish dumps.

Roman and Viking shoes

In Roman Britain, people wore open-work sandals with long laces, and heavy boots with nail-studded soles. Wealthy women wore elegant slippers. Small children wore little lace-up bootees. One man in York was buried with two spare pairs of boots, for use in his next life!

Viking cobblers must have spent a lot of time putting new soles on shoes. Many worn-out soles were found in York. Among the Viking shoes found were ankle-high boots and slip-on shoes.

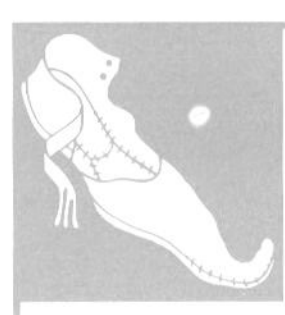

Clues from the Past

Medieval shoes

Hundreds of shoes were found in rubbish dumped behind medieval waterfronts in London. They have given many clues about how shoes were made, and how fashions changed between the twelfth and sixteenth centuries.

In the twelfth century, the upper part of a shoe or boot was cut as one piece of leather, but from the thirteenth century, some were made with a separate piece for the back of the heel. Goatskin was used until about 1250, when calfskin became common.

The upper part of the shoe was sewn to a tough cow-hide sole, and then the shoe was turned inside out, so that the seam was more waterproof. About 1150, shoemakers began to sew a leather strip, the 'rand', between the sole and the upper. From the fifteenth century, an extra outer sole was stitched on to make stouter footwear.

Most people wore short boots that had to be as high as the ankle to keep them on, until between 1250 and 1300 shoemakers discovered that stitching a cord round the edge of the leather stopped it stretching. They could then make low-cut shoes that would stay on the foot. These became very popular for indoor wear.

Out of doors, by 1350 people wore boots that came halfway up the leg and laced up one side. About 1400, short boots that laced at the front had a tongue, like a modern walking shoe.

Trouble with feet

Many shoes show that people had painful feet, with bunions, hammer toes and other conditions. If their shoes felt tight, they cut the leather to stop the shoes hurting the sore places. It saved buying a new pair!

How big were people's feet?

Leather shoes found on excavations have shrunk a little, but allowing for this, archaeologists have worked out foot sizes by measuring the shoes. On Roman and medieval sites in London, all children's sizes corresponding to our sizes 1-13 have been found, showing that children wore shoes as soon as they could walk. For adult shoes, a measurement similar to our size 5 is the commonest, showing that Roman and medieval feet were smaller than ours.

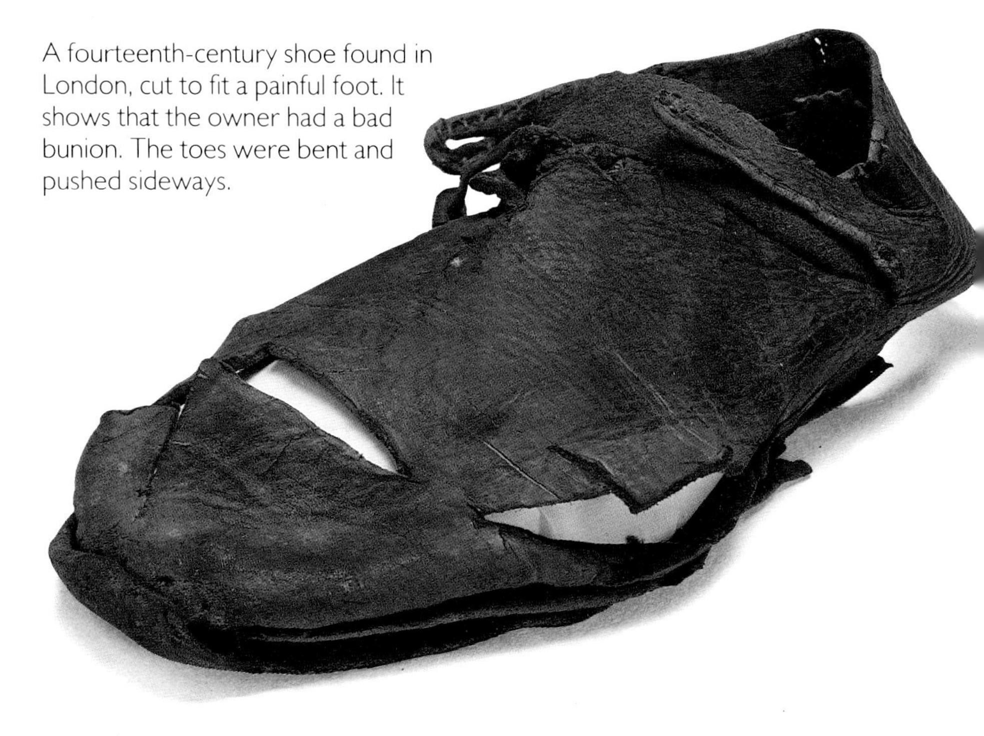

A fourteenth-century shoe found in London, cut to fit a painful foot. It shows that the owner had a bad bunion. The toes were bent and pushed sideways.

Project

Make a medieval poulaine
About 1200, and again about 1370, shoes with very long toes came into fashion. They were called poulaines. Some toes were over 10 cm long and were stuffed with moss to make them stiff. Even some tiny shoes worn by very young children had these fancy toes.

Measure your foot from heel to toe.
Divide your foot measurement by 8 – round up the resulting measurement to a whole number and call this number F.
Draw a grid of 12 by 12 squares, the side of each square measuring the same as F.
Draw the shapes of the four pieces of the shoe on your grid, as shown here.

Materials
Instead of leather, you can use felt or any bits of cloth, with a piece of something thick, like old blanket, for the sole.
Cut out the pieces and sew them together, matching the letters A-E.

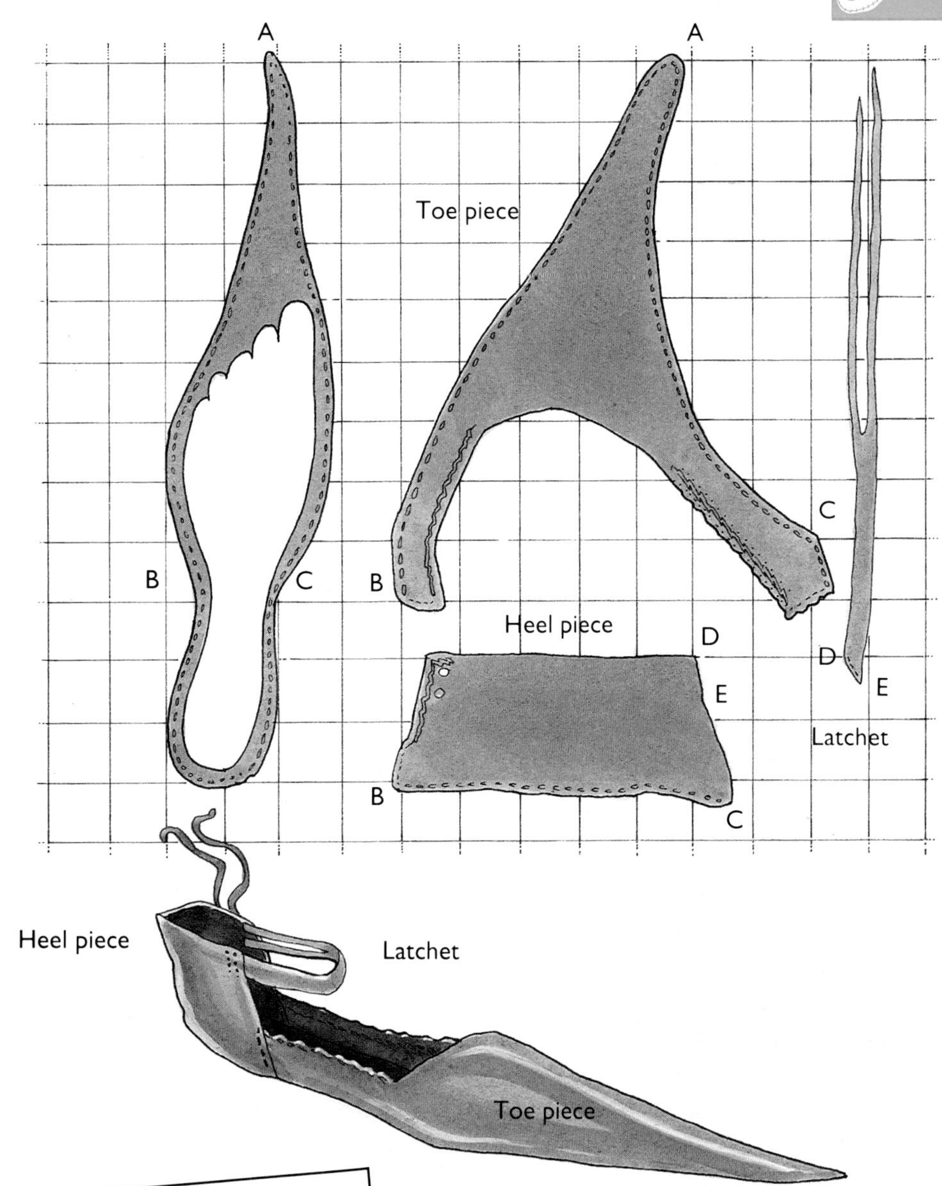

This shoe, made in London, was tied with laces at one side. Patterns are drawn from different shoes to find out how they were made.

A fourteenth-century poulaine and the springy moss that was stuffed in the toe to make it curl up (left). Mosses in shoes found in London came from up to 16 km away, and from Hampstead Heath and Blackheath – a trade in moss!

Pottery

Pots give clues to the skill of the people who made them. In Britain, pots were handmade until the first century BC, when the potter's wheel was introduced.

Neolithic farmers were the first British potters, nearly 7,000 years ago. Their pottery was very well made, much better than the pots made 2,000 years later, which were thick and badly fired. Early Bronze Age beakers were very thin-walled and well decorated. The potters stamped patterns on them with little wooden combs, and were very clever at fitting the designs around the pot so that they did not overlap. Iron Age pots had beautiful curved designs drawn on them.

Some Saxon pots were decorated with patterns made with wooden or bone stamps. Archaeologists have spotted the same stamp used on different pots, and have been able to show which were made by the same potter.

A conservator looking down a magnifier into a Roman pot. Under the earth inside the pot, he found the bones of a sacrificed chicken.

How was it made?

Some pots are interesting because the potters working in clay imitated containers made of wood or leather that have since rotted away. Some Bronze Age beakers imitated wooden tankards. The pattern on the base of certain pottery beakers is like the tree-rings that would have appeared on the bottom of a tankard made of wood.

Archaeologists recognize a wheel-made pot by its regular shape and lines left by the potter's tool on the inside of the pot as it spun round.

How was it used?

Some pots show traces of what was inside them long ago – if diggers don't scrub them off when they are washing the pieces. A black crust in a neolithic pot found on the Isle of Rhum in the Inner Hebrides was analysed in a laboratory. It was the remains of heather ale, made from cereals and herbs. A sample was made up by a whisky manufacturer. It was golden in colour.

Trade long ago

Pottery gives clues to trade between different places. Big jars, called amphorae, were used to bring fish-paste from Spain and wine from Italy to Roman Britain. Archaeologists have discovered where the different shapes of amphorae were made. In the Middle Ages, pottery was imported from France, the Netherlands and Scandinavia. Broken pots from ships' cargoes were dumped at English ports. Archaeologists have found

out where they were made by looking for similar pots in foreign museums.

Saintonge wine jars were made in Gascony (southern France) in the Middle Ages. There are documents from the year 1407 showing that wine was shipped from Gascony to England. But archaeologists have found bits of these jars in England that date from 100 years earlier than 1407, showing that the trade began long before we have written evidence for it.

A wine jug of the kind called Saintonge ware, dug up at Southampton. It came there from France, containing wine. Only rich people could afford these decorated jugs with parrot-beak spout.

Project

Make a Bronze Age beaker
Roll out clay into long sausages and coil them round and round into the shape of this beaker, about 18 cm tall. Smooth the surface with your fingers.

Find a thin piece of wood about 2 cm square. Cut five teeth along the one edge of the wood (ask a grown-up to help you with this). Press the wooden teeth into the clay to decorate your beaker with the same patterns as the person who made this one did 4,500 years ago. The beaker shown above was found at Durrington in Wiltshire.

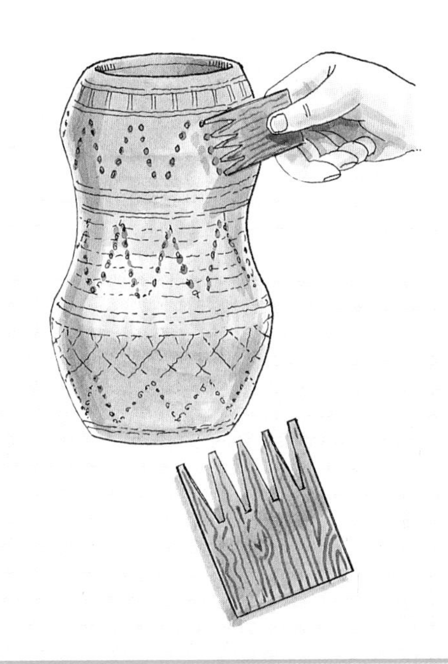

Tiles

The Romans introduced tile-making to Britain. In Roman Britain, tiles were made for roofs, for strengthening stone walls and for central heating systems in homes and bath houses.

Some of the clues found on tiles are not just about the ways they were made and used, but tell us something about the people who made them. After tiles were cut out from sheets of damp clay, they were left to dry on the ground. Many show footprints or paw-marks of cats and dogs. One has the mark of a stone thrown at the animal by an angry tile-maker.

On a tile at Fishbourne Roman Palace, West Sussex, are marks left by a bare foot and the sole of a shoe. Were they made by children playing, perhaps the tile-maker's children?

A tile found at Fishbourne with marks left by a bare foot and one wearing a shoe (above).

Words written on tiles (graffiti) are even more interesting. On a tile found in London, a Roman tile-maker had written: 'Augustalis has been going off on his own every day this fortnight.' Some medieval tiles have words and numbers written on them as instructions to workmen laying the tile floor. These graffiti show that there were Roman and medieval tile-makers who could read and write.

Part of the roof of a building in Roman Britain. Flat tiles, tegulae, were laid side by side. Curved tiles, called imbrices, were laid over the joins to keep out the rain.

A stack of copies of Roman tiles, made for archaeologists to use on a reconstructed Roman building in Germany.

Before chimney stacks were built, smoke curled up into the roof of a house and came out through a ventilator, or louvre. This example from Oxford may represent a jester.

Medieval roof tiles

Covering a roof with tiles instead of thatch made a house safer to live in. There were so many fires in towns from thatched roofs catching fire that in 1212 a law was made ordering everyone in London to have a tiled roof.

Roof tiles were glazed to make them shiny. Some were coloured green or white. Ridge tiles along the top of a roof were decorated with patterns, and clay figures were often placed at each end. The ventilator shown here was used instead of a chimney on a house in Oxford.

Clues from the Past

Medieval floor tiles

Tiles for floors were very expensive, so tiled floors were only laid in churches, castles, palaces and the homes of rich people like merchants. A very large floor of mosaic tiles, and the kiln where they were made, was found at Norton Priory, near Runcorn in Cheshire. Mosaic floor tiles were made in many different shapes fitted together to make a pattern. Cutting out the tiles individually could take a long time. Most mosaic tiles were coloured green or yellow.

Many square tiles were decorated with a pattern made by pressing a carved wooden stamp into the clay. The sunken pattern was filled in with white clay that showed up against the background of red, green, yellow or black.

A square floor tile from Rye, East Sussex, showing King Edward I. It is 138 mm square and 23 mm thick. It was found in a field where clay was dug for tiles (which were fired in kilns). This tile may have been made for a leper hospital in AD 1290.

Project

Making medieval floor tiles

The pattern shown here, which you can recreate in clay, is a mosaic tile border from a floor excavated at Rievaulx Abbey, Yorkshire.

Medieval tile-makers used templates (pattern pieces) made of lead as a guide to cutting out the sections of the border pattern. You can make similar templates out of cardboard, following the instructions below.

The section shown here is part of a repeat pattern, which means if you make two or more sets of the tiles, the shapes will join up. The instructions below are for making the tiles in clay. If you haven't any clay, you can make your tile sets out of thick cardboard and paint them in the same colours.

Cutting the templates

Using a pencil, draw a rectangle 18× 14 cm on thick cardboard. Measure off 2 cm at top and bottom, leaving a 14 cm square in the middle.

With compasses set to 7 cm, draw arcs of a circle from points A, B, C and D, at the corners of the square.

With compasses set to 2 cm, draw a semi-circle in the centre of the top and bottom sides, at points E and F.

Rub out the lines AB and CD. Cut out your seven templates.

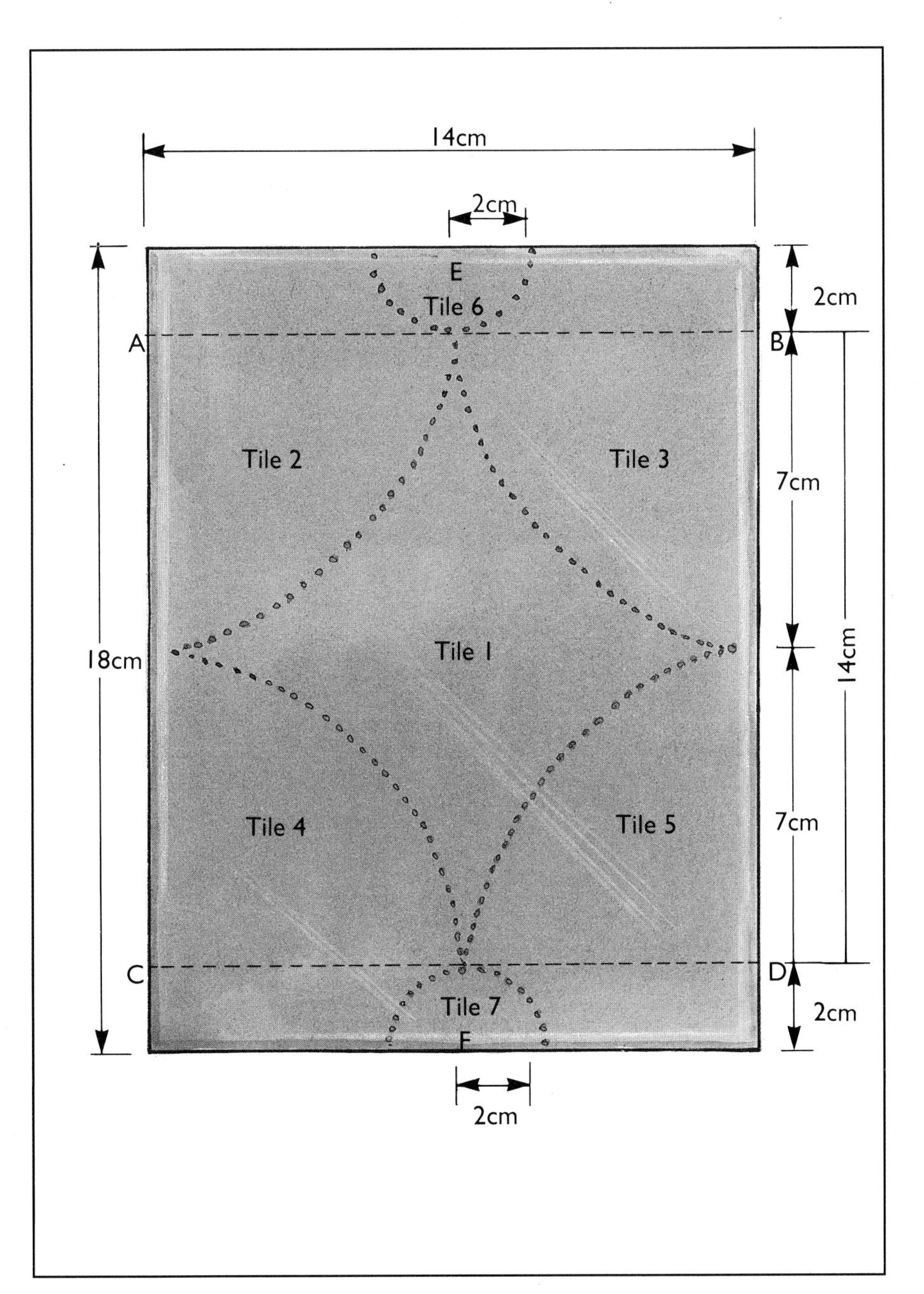

Cutting the tiles

To make the tiles, it is easiest to use modelling clay that hardens without firing, which you can buy in a craft shop. You can paint the tiles as soon as they have dried completely. Or, if you are able to use a pottery kiln during an art class, you can use clay that has to be fired – ask a teacher to help you.

Roll out the clay with a rolling pin until it measures at least 18×14 cm and is 2 cm thick. Leave the clay to get firm, but do not let it dry out completely.

Place one of your templates on the clay and use a thick needle to prick holes along the edges, so the shape is marked on the clay. Fit the next shape to the first one, and prick the lines as before. Repeat with each template until you have marked the whole pattern on the clay.

Take off the templates and cut carefully along the dots to separate the clay tiles. Let them dry until they are hard. Then colour the tiles by painting the upper surfaces – if you are going to fire your tiles in a kiln, you need to use coloured glazes instead of paint.

Kilns

The oldest pots in Britain were fired in a bonfire to make them hard, as they still are in some parts of the world. But by the Iron Age, potters used clay and stone to build a roof over the fire to make a kiln, like an oven.

Clay has to be fired (baked in intense heat) not only to harden it, but to make it waterproof and long-lasting. Objects such as cups, jars and roof tiles must be water-resistant. Using a kiln, a potter could fire pots at a higher temperature than in a bonfire, and let air in or keep it away from the pots, to make them cream-coloured, or red or black.

Archaeologists have built reconstructions of kilns like some that have been excavated, and fired pots and tiles in them to get exact copies of ancient ones. One experiment found that a Romano-British kiln used up 250 kg of wood for the firing and reached a temperature of 800 °C.

A major find

At a dig in Lyveden, Northamptonshire, archaeologists found evidence of the whole process of pot-making in about AD1200; the puddling pits where clay was mixed, the workshops where pots were shaped, and the sheds where pots were left to dry before firing, as well as the kilns themselves. By examining the remains of charcoal, they found that wood from oak, field maple, hazel, ash and blackthorn trees had been burnt to heat the kilns. They even found the knives and bone tools the potters had used.

A medieval tile kiln

Many medieval kilns have been excavated, but nobody knew what a kiln for firing mosaic floor tiles looked like, until Mrs Elizabeth Eames excavated one at Meaux, Yorkshire, in 1957. It was difficult to find clues, as this kiln had been broken up, and a kiln for firing square tiles had been built on top of it. Because mosaic tiles are made in different shapes, they are more difficult to stack in a kiln than square tiles.

First the remains of the square-tile kiln were

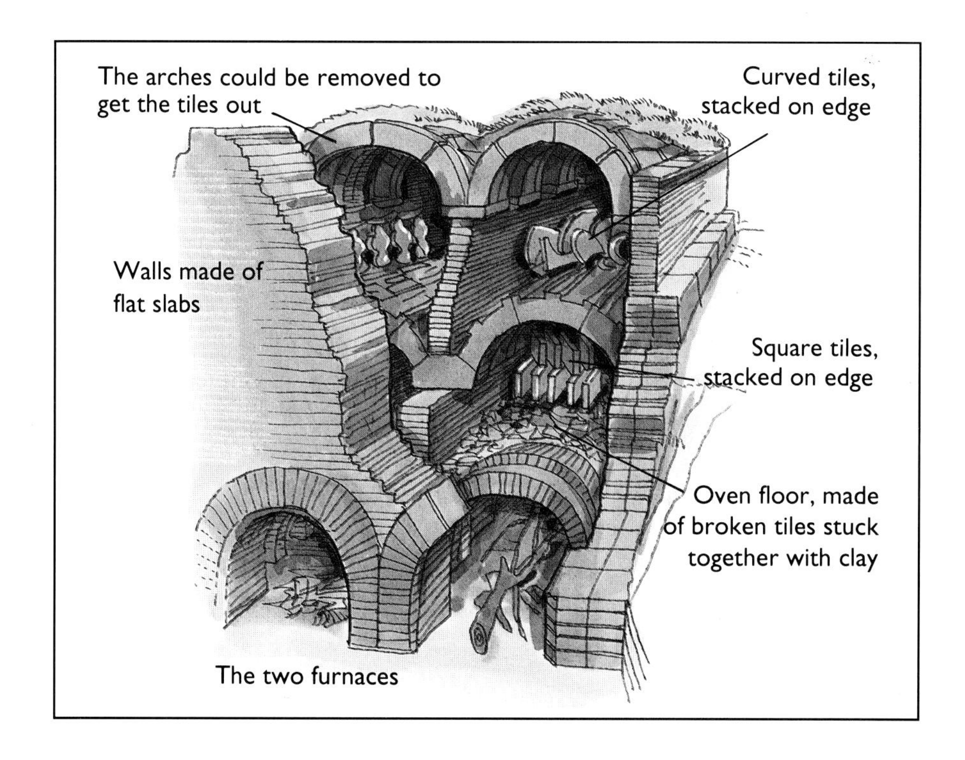

A reconstruction of the kiln for firing mosaic tiles found at Meaux Abbey.

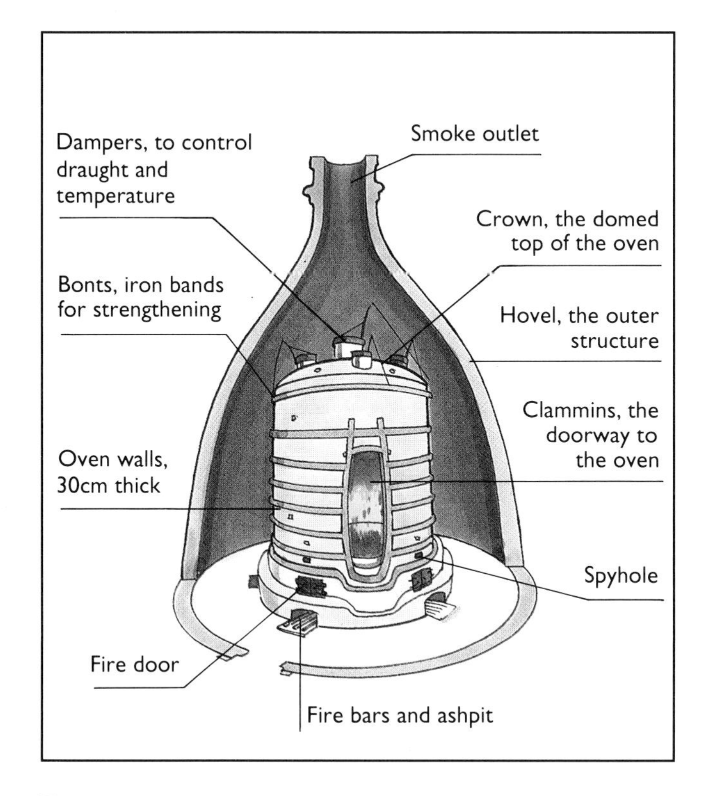

The diagram (above) shows the inside of a bottle kiln, with the oven where the china was fired. The picture (right) shows a bottle kiln in Ironbridge.

excavated and cleared away. Then Mrs Eames found clay pieces used in building the earlier kiln. There were flat bricks from the walls, and curved ones from the arches. Curved slabs had been used to make removable shelves in the upper part.

Mrs Eames knew that mosaic tiles had been fired in this kiln as she found 'wasters', bits of tiles that had stuck to others and had been thrown away. A drawing of what the kiln must have been like was made from all the clues found at the dig.

Industrial kilns

In the Middle Ages, pots were traded only in the local area of the kiln where they were made, because transporting them was difficult. In the eighteenth century, large kilns were built that used coal to fire hundreds of pots at a time, at temperatures of up to 1,350 °C. Josiah Wedgwood of North Staffordshire was one of the first potters to realize that he could sell a lot more of his wares if they could be carried quickly, and in big loads, to other parts of England and to ports, to be sold overseas. He supported the building of new roads and helped to pay for a canal linking the River Trent with the River Mersey. This made a waterway 150 km long across the Midlands.

With these improved transport systems, all the potters in North Staffordshire found that they could sell more of their wares. So many kilns were built that this area of England became known as 'the Potteries'. There are few of the huge bottle-shaped kilns left today. They have been replaced by modern gas-fired kilns.

Buildings

Much archaeological work involves getting information from ancient things buried in the ground. But some archaeologists study buildings that stand above ground.

These buildings may be only one or two hundred years old, not 'old' compared with many things described in this book. But we have to think of providing information for people who will live in the thirtieth and fortieth centuries! To them, the eighteenth century and the Victorian era will seem like ancient history.

Many old buildings are demolished to make way for new roads, car parks and shopping precincts. Old factories are replaced by modern ones. We don't want our country to become a huge museum, so some old buildings have to go. Archaeologists try to describe and photograph important ones.

Part of the wall that stood around Roman London, found on a building site during modern redevelopment in the City of London.

Preserving the past

Parts of the city wall of Roman London have been discovered while building sites were being cleared. Some developers preserve ancient structures in their new buildings, as in the plan for a new office block shown here, which is designed to keep a length of the Roman wall so that people can see it.

One way of avoiding the need to demolish old buildings is to give them a new function. Then they will remain in good repair, for people in the future to see. This is the case at the fifteenth-century church of Saint Saviour's in York.

The diagram (above) is for a new building enclosing a section of London's Roman wall (on the left of the picture).
The picture (above right) shows the old church forming the Archaeological Resource Centre in York.

The church now houses the Archaeological Resource Centre, a museum where visitors can actually take part in archaeological work.

Industrial archaeology
Many industrial processes began in Britain in the eighteenth century. Technical achievements made during the period known as the Industrial Revolution spread all over the world. In the 1960s, industrial archaeologists began to record buildings constructed in the Industrial Revolution, and the machines inside them. Although many factories were described when they were built, and we have plans of them and catalogues illustrating what they made, many documents were thrown away, or don't tell us all we need to know. Excavation of important sites where buildings were demolished provides further clues.

Abraham Darby's Old Furnace being cleared in 1950. The waterwheel was on the left. The molten iron ran out of the fore arch in the centre.

A famous ironworks

The Old Furnace at Coalbrookdale, Shropshire, is one of the most interesting industrial sites in the world. In this blast furnace, in 1709, Abraham Darby used coke instead of charcoal to smelt iron ore and produce cast iron. Using coke meant that much more cast iron could be produced, at a time when wood for charcoal was in short supply. Darby's idea spread to other ironworks, first in Britain, then in other countries.

It was in this furnace that huge girders were cast for the famous Iron Bridge over the River Severn – the first bridge in the world to be constructed from iron.

The furnace was eventually outdated, and in 1818 it was abandoned. Archaeologists found clay pipes of that date in the slag and rubble that covered up the Old Furnace, when later ironworks were built over the ruins.

In 1950, Allied Iron-founders Ltd, who make Raeburn cast iron stoves at Coalbrookdale, decided to clear the old buildings away and extend their factory.

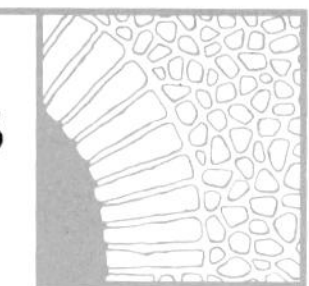

Luckily, they knew where the Old Furnace was and had it cleared so it could be photographed before it was removed. But so much of the Old Furnace was standing that the company decided to celebrate its 250th anniversary in 1959 by preserving what remained. The Old Furnace was completely excavated, and is now protected by a glass building. Children from a Sheffield school made and presented a working model of the furnace to help visitors understand the remains.

The Iron Bridge, constructed with girders made in Darby's Old Furnace.

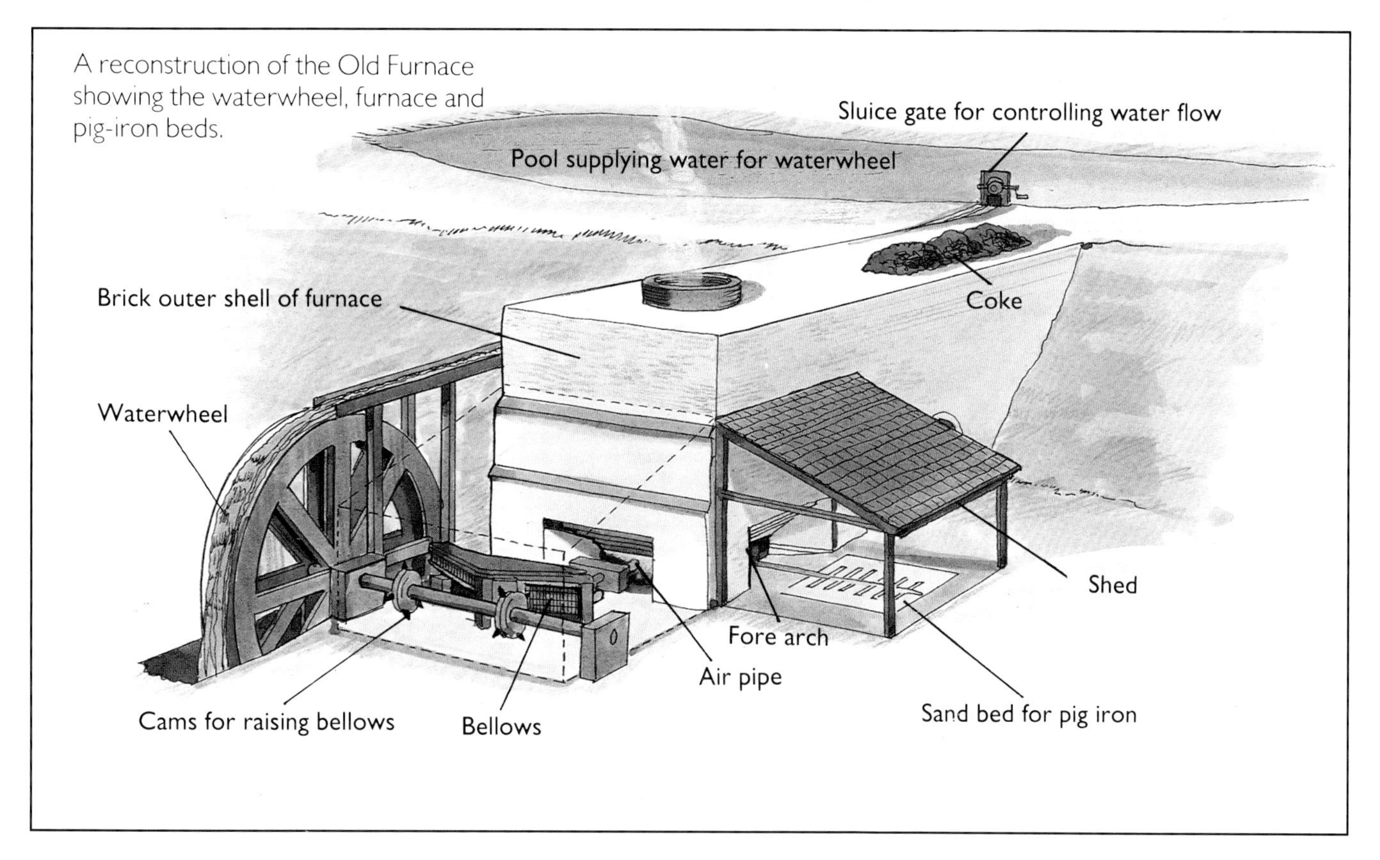

A reconstruction of the Old Furnace showing the waterwheel, furnace and pig-iron beds.

Glossary

Archaeology The study of how people lived a long time ago.
Bronze Age The years between 2500 BC and 600 BC in Britain, when bronze was the metal mostly used to make tools, before the introduction of ironworking.
Cartilage Tough white gristle in the skeleton, much of it becoming bone as a child grows up.
Celt The Celts were a prehistoric people who lived in central and western Europe.
Cesspit A hole in the ground, dug to hold excrement from lavatories.
Corrosion Damage to a material caused by moisture and chemical reactions. This can occur through long exposure to the air or burial in the ground. Corrosion takes different forms, typically making a discoloured coating on the surface of the material, like the rust that forms on iron.
Dig An excavation by archaeologists.
Excavation Digging down into the ground to uncover evidence of the past that has been buried. On an excavation, archaeologists examine all the layers of ground, from the modern surface down to natural, undisturbed soil or bedrock.
Find An object found during excavation.
Hammer toes Toes bent right over, through wearing badly fitting shoes.
Implement A tool.
Industrial Revolution The time from 1760 to the early nineteenth century, when mechanical inventions allowed the growth of big industries in factories.
Kiln A special oven for firing pottery and tiles to make them hard.
Leprosy A disease that has various effects including damage to the nerves, so that people cannot feel when they are touched even by something very hot.
Loom A machine for weaving yarn into cloth.
Manuscript A document written by hand.
Medieval Belonging to the Middle Ages.
Mesolithic The time between about 9000 BC and 4000 BC in Britain, when people started making more complicated tools and weapons using small flakes of flint, sometimes set in bone or wooden handles.
Middle Ages The time between 1066 and 1485 in Britain, when most people worked on the land.
Milk teeth A child's first set of small teeth, that are replaced by larger, permanent teeth as the jaws grow.
Molar teeth Large back teeth that crush food.
Mosaic A pattern of tiles of different shapes, used as floor covering in the Middle Ages. In Roman Britain, mosaic floors were made with tiny square pieces of coloured stones.
Neolithic The time between about 4000 BC and 2500 BC in Britain, when farming and pottery-making were introduced from mainland Europe.
Palaeolithic The time when people first began to make very simple tools of wood, from around 2.5 to 3 million years ago up until 12,000 to 10,000 BC.
Parchment The skin of sheep or goats, treated to make a dry material for writing on.
Puddling Mixing hard clay with water to make it soft enough to shape into pots.
Radioactive carbon atoms Unstable carbon atoms which give out energy as they break down. The energy given out is called radiation. Carbon atoms are found in all living things.
Radiocarbon method This dating method relies on the fact that living things absorb radioactive carbon atoms when alive, but stop absorbing them when they die. The radioactive carbon atoms break down at a steady rate, so by measuring the amount of radiocarbon atoms left in an old piece of wood scientists can work out its age.
Romano-Briton A person who lived in Britain when the country was part of the Roman Empire.
Saxon Saxons were people from northern Europe who invaded Britain in the fourth and fifth centuries AD and set up their own kingdoms, which became England.
Stone Age The period before people discovered metalworking. It is divided into three periods: palaeolithic, mesolithic, and neolithic – see entries.
Tanned The description of animal skins treated by soaking them in pits with water and oak bark, to make leather. The process is called tanning.
Thatch Bundles of straw or reeds used to make a roof.
Tuberculosis A disease, usually in the lungs, that spreads among people living in overcrowded houses.
Turves Lumps of grass growing in earth, cut out of the ground and used for building walls or a mound.
Unleavened bread Flat loaves made without yeast, so the dough has not risen.
Vikings Warriors and traders from Norway, Sweden, Denmark and Iceland, who raided Britain in the eighth to eleventh centuries and fought to get land for their own kingdoms.
Waterfront A wooden wall built out in a river with a bank of rubbish filling the wet ground behind it. Ships could stay in deep water and tie up to the wall to unload their cargoes.
X-ray photograph A picture which reveals what lies underneath the surface of an object. X-rays can pass through some solid things.

Places to visit

At the Archaeological Resource Centre in York you can see and assist archaeologists at work on finds from excavations.

At these places, you can see reconstructed houses and workplaces.
Flag Fen Visitor Centre, Fengate, Peterborough, Cambridgeshire (Bronze Age village and farm).
Butser Ancient Farm, Queen Elizabeth Country Park, Petersfield, Hampshire.
Somerset Levels and Moors Visitor Centre, The Willows Garden Centre, Westhay, Somerset (prehistoric trackways and farming).
Vindolanda, Chesterholm Museum, Bardon Hill, Hexham (a Roman fort).
The White Cliffs Experience, Dover (the Roman invasion, and life in Kent up to the Second World War).
The Weald and Downland Open Air Museum, Singleton, West Sussex (reconstructions of medieval houses).
The Darby Furnace and the Museum of Iron, Ironbridge Gorge, Telford, Shropshire.
The Shipwreck Heritage Centre, Hastings, East Sussex.
The Mary Rose Trust, Portsmouth, Hampshire.
The Great Orme Coppermines, Llandudno, North Wales (Bronze Age mines).
The Ulster History Park, Omagh, Co. Tyrone.
The Irish National Heritage Park, Ferrycarrig, Co. Wexford.

Books to read

Younger children may need help in getting information from these books.

Eames, E. English *Medieval Tiles* (British Museum, 1992)
Lubin, H. *The Worcester Pilgrim* (Worcester Cathedral Publications No.1, 1990) – (Reconstruction of costume from a burial)
McIntosh, J. *Archaeology* (Dorling Kindersley, 1994)
Place, R. *Bodies from the Past* (Wayland, 1995)
Medieval Britain (Wayland, 1989)
Romans – Fact & Fiction (CUP, 1988)
Vikings – Fact & Fiction (CUP, 1985)
Stead, I. *Celtic Art* (British Museum, 1985)

Index

Page numbers in **bold** refer to illustrations as well as text.